BRING THEM IN!

BRING THEM IN!

Bob Harrington

"The Chaplain of Bourbon Street"

BROADMAN PRESS
Nashville, Tennessee

4255-44

ISBN: 0-8054-5544-2
Dewey Decimal classification: 269
Library of Congress catalog card number: 74-77358
Printed in the United States of America

Preface

This is going to be a book about soul-winning; about soul-winning methods; about soul-winners; about soul-winning experiences.

I have not tried to develop the contents of this book where one chapter grows from another. I have rather tried to arrange the contents so that wherever a person begins reading—in the middle or at the end—he will go straight to the heart of the matter—the exciting, often discouraging, but always rewarding effort to bring people to Jesus.

I am a preacher second and a soul-winner first. I don't believe in second-hand religion. Nor do I believe in second-hand witnessing. No Christian can pass to another his own responsibility to witness for Christ.

It is hoped that every chapter in this book will contain both information and inspiration. The most important thing I can offer on the subject of soul-winning is the 16 years of trying to reach people personally every day.

Frankly, the only thing it takes to become a soul-winner is the willingness to try. I can't recall a single day in the last 16 years when I didn't try to witness to someone about Christ.

Therefore, my one desire is that you who read this book will catch the idea that soul-winning is not the task of a favored few, but is supposed to be as much a part of the life-style of every Christian as eating and sleeping.

Contents

1

"Bringatation"

People have said I am full of holy boldness. I like that tag because I am convinced that the basic ingredient of an effective witness is courage. I don't spend a lot of time trying to teach people how to become soul-winners. I simply try to motivate people to give it a try. I think if God were to send a special invitation to heaven today, it would read, "Come and bring a friend."

Getting My Wife to Witness

I remember when I was first saved and started witnessing and telling people about my experience with the Lord. I wanted my wife to go with me visiting.

Joyce always felt reluctant because she thought maybe she didn't know what to say, or wasn't qualified to talk for the Lord.

I said, "Come with me. Let's go together and talk about what the Lord has done for our home. Talk about your life as a teenager and when you gave your heart to the Lord. Tell them how you refused, at first, to serve the Lord like you should. This would be a fantastic witness!"

So my wife went with me to visit people. The first thing she knew, she started talking; she started communicating—sharing her witness with others. She told of her trials with me as a lost man—both husband and daddy—and how she failed to talk to me about

9

her experience with the Lord. She began to share her witness with me; to pray in front of me and share her concern for me. She even had people praying for me although I didn't know it.

Joyce made a far greater impression on me than she realized. Don't ever hesitate to try to bring those you love to the Lord.

Fred Roan—Auto Dealer in Mobile

A lot of people tell me they aren't good at talking. This is no excuse for failing to witness for Christ. A person doesn't have to have a college degree to be an effective witness for Christ. All it takes to witness for Christ is a heart to care and a spirit to try.

Fred Roan, a car dealer in Mobile, Alabama, meant so much to my early years of serving the Lord. He was a man who didn't complete grade school. Fred had an experience with the Lord as a grown businessman, and took his ability to sell cars and converted it to an ability to witness for the Lord.

Here's a man who couldn't spell a word with two syllables much less pronounce them correctly. But when Fred fell in love with the Lord, his witness was more a part of his conversation than the current events of the day.

This man talked to people about the Lord in the car lot, the restaurant, or riding down the road. I remember one experience when I was first saved. Fred stopped at a traffic light and witnessed to people who were waiting at the bus stop. At the time, this really scared me. You read today about my boldness, when I am 16 years old in Christ. But when I was first saved, this man with such boldness scared me.

Fred not only scared me, he also attracted me with his concern, compassion, and stickability as he would share his faith and let people know what Christ meant to him.

Fred was a "Bringer." He used to bring people with him to church, to Christian Businessmen's meetings, and other opportunities of witness. I know many people who are saved today, not because Fred Roan and Bob Harrington were able to lead them to the Lord right on the spot, but because we took them to a place where someone else could help them. They watered the seed that Fred and I planted and God gave the increase. We all rejoiced together.

Bringatation is a fantastic way to reach people for Christ. There will be many people you cannot reach face-to-face or heart-to-heart. But you will be able to bring them to a situation where they can be reached.

I thank God that I had the opportunity to spend so much time with a "bringer" like Fred Roan early in my Christian life. He was a soul-winner then and will always be a soul-winner. I think the first thing Fred Roan will do when he steps into heaven will be to check out those who are still outside but just within reach of the gate. He may surprise me and say, "Well, my witnessing days are over because I'm up here now with the King of kings and the Lord of lords."

My Dad with His Bicycling Club

Maybe you have convinced yourself that you can't put the right words together to talk to someone about Jesus. I really do not go along with that. The word "witness" simply means telling someone what has happened to you. Anybody ought to be able to tell what happened to him. An apologist is a defender of the faith. He is the one who needs to know all of the Bible verses and theology and history and all of that. But a witness simply needs to know what happened to him. A witness simply needs to be able to tell what he has seen and heard and felt. This is the reason why an eight-year-old child can be a witness, because he can tell what he has seen and heard and experienced.

Three days after my conversion I had the opportunity to win my mother to faith in Christ. It took fifteen days to get my daddy. My daddy was reluctant right at first because he didn't want me to push anything on him or to take him along too fast. He was excited about what happened to me but he didn't know whether he was ready to go this "holy route" or not.

He had always been a good man as far as I can remember. Morally he was good. Financially he was always able to provide what my brother and I needed.

And yet, fifteen days after my conversion I had the opportunity to lead him to the Lord. At the writing of this book, my daddy is the pastor of a Methodist church in Brent, Alabama where, for eight years, he has been serving the Lord. I just talked with him on the phone a few days ago and one of his newest projects is bicycling for his health. In addition to just riding to keep his body in good tone, he has developed a little gang of bicycle riders. These are teenagers who ride along with him. My dad, incidentally, is in his seventies.

In all this riding, his real motive is to bring these kids to Jesus! To some, he witnesses while they are riding—person to person. Most of them, he simply encourages to come to church or Sunday School. He tells me he wants these young people to feel the presence and power of the Holy Spirit.

Isn't this fascinating? It doesn't really matter whether you are down on Bourbon Street or pastoring a church in a little country town in Alabama. It doesn't matter whether you are riding around in a Trailways Silver Eagle Bus, as I do, going now from town to town or pedaling around on a bicycle with kids. You can always be giving your witness for the purpose of bringing people to Jesus. The thought of bringing people to Jesus is fantastic. When I think back over my experiences with the Lord and the experiences I have week by week in crusades across America, I thank God that I have the opportunity to bring people to Jesus Christ.

General Butler Brought His Banker

Let's assume, for the moment, that you cannot talk adequately enough as far as you are concerned to tell someone how to become a Christian. If you are in that condition, what should you do? The answer is simple. You should bring that person to someone who can do the talking.

On one of my crusades in Nashville, Tennessee, I had the opportunity to win General Howard Butler to the Lord. General Butler is a two-star general, retired from the United States Air Force and former commanding general of the Tennessee Air National

Guard. General Butler is an outstanding attorney, practicing law today with a firm that is known throughout the south. When the general first came to hear me preach, he got under conviction. He began to ask himself, "What alibi will I use?" His legalistic mind naturally gravitated toward a way in which he could justify his sinful condition when he stood before the Lord. He knew when he stood before the Lord Jesus Christ—the Judge in charge of the Supreme of all Supreme Courts—the Utopia of all Judgeships—that he would have no excuse. He knew he would have to face the Lord one day as certain as anyone else who ever breathed a breath of God's kindness. So the general was convicted of the fact that he had no alibi and he gave his heart and life to Jesus Christ.

I can still remember that night in his home when we knelt down with some friends and I had the joy of taking my Bible and leading General Howard Butler into the army of Jesus Christ.

Immediately after his conversion, he began testifying. He appeared with me on television. He appeared at our crusades. He started telling his neighbors and friends about what happened to him. At this particular time, he was so new in the Lord he could command thousands of people in the military, but he couldn't command his ability to win someone to the Lord. So the next best thing for him was to bring people to me so that I could reach them for the Lord.

I remember one night, after preaching, I went down to the basement of an adjoining church for some refreshment and fellowship with God's people. General Butler came running over to me. You would never picture a general like this, coming up to a preacher and saying, "Brother Bob, here is a man who needs to be right with the Lord. He is a good friend of mine—a banker—and has a great reputation in this city. He just needs to do what I did. He needs to lose his religion and find Christ!"

I said, "All right, I surely will be praying for this man."

The general said, "No, he needs what I'm talking about right now! Right now, Bob, we better stop what you are doing and pray! This man is ready!"

I remember how persistent he was and how we all got down

on our knees right there in the fellowship hall of this church. This banker who had been surrounded by religion gave his heart and life to the Lord Jesus Christ. After we prayed, this man stood up, rejoicing with his experience. The general was rejoicing also and we had revival right there in the basement because a general brought another man to Jesus.

In the second chapter of Mark, there is a beautiful story. Four men had a sick friend. Obviously, one man could not carry the bed by himself, but four of them could. So the four men took their sick friend in a bundle and picked him up and carried him along the road. They knew that their friend needed Jesus. They began the process of searching for Jesus.

Why were they so anxious to find Jesus? Because they didn't know what to tell this man. They couldn't think of the word that would help him. They didn't know what to say to get the man right. But they knew that if they could only find Jesus, that their friend would have help.

The Bible says that there was a crowd where Jesus was preaching. In fact, there was a big crowd. In fact, they could not even get near Jesus. But these men would not be discouraged.

Recently, I preached in Del City, Oklahoma. From the very first night, the crowds were overwhelming. We filled the auditorium, filled the overflow rooms, and finally turned about one thousand people away. I can't tell you how it pained me to stand in that parking lot and watch cars drive away because there literally was not a way to get into the preaching service. This is the reason why I have to go to coliseums today. It costs a lot of money to go into a coliseum. And often a big crowd doesn't look quite as large in a big coliseum. But it breaks my heart to think about people being turned away.

The Bible says there was such a big crowd, these men couldn't even get through the door. The men looked around and said, "Well, let's take him to the window." They went around to the windows and they couldn't even see inside. They said, "Well, what are we going to do?" If this had been a group of modern day comfort-oriented, twentieth-century Christians, they would have dropped the bed and said, "Let's come back another day." Instead, one of them said, "I'll tell you what we are going to do; we'll put him up on the roof."

Two of the men got up on top of the roof and lifted while the other two men stood on the ground and pushed. Finally, they got the sick man up on the roof. They proceeded to tear a hole in the roof. Can you imagine how large a hole they had to tear in that house in order to have one large enough to drop a bed down through it? They looked down and the crowd was so entranced by what Jesus was saying that they didn't even notice that half the roof was gone. So the four men began to lower the man right down to the feet of Jesus. And if you will take the time to look in your Bible at the second chapter of Mark and the fifth verse, you will see one of the most powerful verses of Scripture in all the Bible. Listen to what Jesus said: "When Jesus saw *their* faith, he said unto the sick of the palsy, Son, thy sins be forgiven thee."

Did you catch whose faith made this man forgiven? It wasn't the sick man's faith that Jesus honored. It was the faith of those four men who had lowered him down through the roof!

Jesus figured that if these four men were willing to work that hard, he was going to honor their faith. This man who was sick, got his sins forgiven and we don't even know if he had any faith at all. I'm sure he got faith. Because Jesus gave it to him. That's how any of us get faith. Jesus gives it to us. I'm sure the sick man later came to a faith in Jesus. But the thing that got him down the road to Jesus was not his own faith, but the faith of those who brought him.

That's why it's important to bring people to Jesus. *Your* faith can make *them* well. Your faith can get their sins forgiven. Your faith can get that other person on the road to Jesus.

Recently, my family and I were guests of Rex Humbard as we went to visit the Land of the Bible. It was my first trip to The Holy Land. While I was there, I felt a closeness to the Lord I had never known before. I experienced a total dedication and surrender of myself to the lordship of Christ. I've always loved the Lord and enjoyed being saved. I've always felt that I was spirit-filled and spirit-led on many occasions. But, walking where Jesus walked and standing where he stood and preaching where he preached had a profound impression upon my life. I realized that I could live closer to the Lord day by day.

With this new dedication, I determined to add to our crusade services a special prayer time where people could come for prayer. If they wanted prayer for their body, they could ask for it. If they wanted prayer for their soul, they could ask for it. If they wanted prayer for their marriage, they could ask for it. If they wanted prayer for their family, they could ask for it. I wanted a time in our crusade services when people could come and ask of God whatever they would.

Obviously, this prayer time would also be a time to bring people to Jesus. I now say in our prayer times, "Listen, woman, even if your husband isn't here tonight, bring him to Jesus anyway." You don't know what a thrill it is to have someone come to our altar at prayer time and say to me, "Brother Bob, my son isn't here tonight but, by faith, I am bringing him to Jesus." This special prayer time has proven to be one of the most marvelous things that ever occurred in our crusades. I have seen young people bring their parents to the Lord on a Monday night *by faith*, and before the end of the week, their mother and dad would find Christ.

I've seen wives come forward at special prayer time on Monday, Tuesday, and Wednesday nights. By Saturday night, their husband would be down there with them receiving Christ as Savior. These people brought their loved ones to Jesus by faith even in the absence of the person they were bringing. The presence of the Lord is what honored their faith.

Isn't that a thrilling truth to know? God will honor our faith in helping other people. And isn't it marvelous to know that you can still bring people to Christ even if the people you are bringing are not actually there?

Try to bring your friends and loved ones to a preaching service where they can hear the gospel. But if they won't come with you, don't lose heart. Just go ahead and bring them anyway by faith. Just go down in the name of the Lord for this person and intercede for this person at prayer time. You can be sure that Jesus is at the right hand of God interceding for you and me. You can be sure that he will honor your faith. I've seen, in this special prayer time, someone come forward to pray for another person on the opposite side of the building. And I have watched as, before that prayer time was over, the person for whom they were praying, would be at the altar.

In another place in the Bible, there was a man named Philip who found Christ. The Bible said that as soon as Philip found Christ, he went and found Nathanael and *brought him to Jesus.*

I am going to give you a formula for witnessing that every Christian can do. Here are three things. We've all talked about visitation, which implies going out to find someone and telling about Jesus. I call this formula, "Bringatation." Here are three things that any Christian can do: (1) Bring someone to a preaching service. (2) Sit beside them. (3) Pray for them—God will do the rest.

Now look at those three things. Is there any one of those three that is too difficult for you to do? How much talent does it take to be able to bring someone to a preaching service? How much knowledge do you have to have to be able to sit beside them? How much does it cost you to sit there and pray for them? Anybody can do these three things. And I promise you God will do the rest.

God never intended that other people would be saved by our eloquent words. But He does expect us to do our part. We may not all be able to preach like Paul or Peter, but we can all bring someone to Jesus like those four men did.

This is why I go to large auditoriums and coliseums. I want to make it as easy as possible for other people to bring their friends.

I was saved in 1958. I gave my heart and life to Jesus in a church in Alabama. I did not go to that little church that night to get converted. I went with some other motives that were not that worthy. I didn't know that I needed to be saved. But the fact is that the results turned out that night to be spiritual.

This is the reason I go into auditoriums, coliseums, state fairs, entertainment centers, night clubs, and taverns across America. People will come to an auditorium where they have gone to basketball games or wrestling matches or dances and they will come there because they feel a little more relaxed in that atmosphere. In other words, it's easier to bring people to places like that. This is where I believe we can get people to come and hear the witness and hear a testimony for Christ. It doesn't matter whether or not it's a church, as long as a person can feel the convicting power of the Holy Spirit upon their heart and see their need for Christ as Savior.

I have found that it is much easier to invite people to come to a neutral place than it would be for Baptists to invite a Catholic or a Catholic to invite a Baptist to come to their own particular church building. This is a part of my program of bringatation. I want to help make it as easy as possible to bring people to Christ. I think it is to our advantage to make available situations that will be easy for people to find the Lord. Why should we make it any more difficult than it already is? A person has the guilt of sin stored up in his heart. The person has dozens of years of pride stored up in his heart. The person has many things that are going to have to be changed in his life when he comes to Christ. There are so many other things that make it difficult. Why should we make it more difficult? Why should we not make it easy to bring people to Jesus? Paul always went where people were and directed attention to where people could find his Lord and Savior. This is why I believe in exposing the witness for Christ in places so that people can get at it easy.

I met a man in Oklahoma who was so shy he said he couldn't say his own name in public. He was a Christian only the last two years of his life. He was a relatively unknown man. He was a shoe cobbler by trade.

When this man died, the church was literally packed for his funeral. I asked the pastor of the church how it was that a man who had only been a Christian two years and a member of his church for a little less than that, could fill that huge auditorium? The explanation was that a few years before, this man's pastor had given him the challenge to bring people to church, sit beside them and pray for them. The man did not have even a high school education, but he decided that he could bring people, sit beside them, and pray for them. He had made a practice through the last two years of his life of trying to bring someone with him to church every Sunday; sit beside them and pray for them. The result was that an entire army of people had found Christ by the time this man died.

I like to talk to people about Jesus. I live to do it. I can't remember the day in the past fifteen years when I didn't talk to someone about Jesus. But I'll tell you this; if I couldn't talk to people about Jesus, I would find somebody who could. And I would bring the unsaved to that person.

If you don't think you're good at visitation, why not try bringatation? If you don't feel like telling someone about Jesus, take them to someone who can tell them about Jesus. If you don't know how to preach, then take them to somewhere they can hear preaching. Sit beside them and pray for them. God has promised that he'll do his part. As long as we get people to Jesus, it doesn't really matter who does the talking.

2

Watch a Woman Bring Them

In the fourth chapter of John, there is a beautiful story that we call "The woman at the well." That's not a good title for that chapter, because that woman spent most of her time coming to the well, going away from the well, and coming back to the well. Since we're living in a day when women are being liberated, I want to start this book by using a woman who outwitnessed an entire group of men who were supposed to be the closest followers that Jesus had.

Christ and his disciples were on their way to Galilee. In other words, he was going from the southern part of Palestine up to the northern part. Now, most of the time, Jewish people didn't go straight through Samaria; they would cross over the river and go around Samaria and then cross back over the river and come into Galilee.

Jesus Christ didn't have an ounce of prejudice in his body. He went straight through Samaria. While he was traveling with his disciples, they paused at Jacob's well. Jesus was tired and sat down to rest and, while he rested, the Scripture says that the disciples went into town to get some food.

And the Bible says that while the disciples were on their way into town for groceries, "There cometh a woman of Samaria to draw water." This woman was coming out to the well.

When she got to the well, the disciples were already gone. Obviously, they had met each other on the way into town while the woman was coming out. There was a large number of disciples and the path was probably not very large. Since women were not liberated during those days, I'm quite sure that they made the woman step off the path and let them get on toward their very important job of buying groceries. After they passed, she stepped back on the path and came to the well.

When she got there, Jesus talked to her at great length. Every time she raised some issue, Jesus would bring it back to her own spiritual condition. She talked about water and he talked about the Water of life. She talked about which mountain you should worship and Jesus talked about God being Spirit. He began to talk to her about her own private personal life and ultimately brought her to a point of spiritual revelation. He let her know that he was there to help with her soul.

Jesus Christ was the master soul-winner. He had a way of running along beside anything that someone said and bringing it around to the main point. He always got through to the spiritual need of an individual and that's just what he did with this woman who was saved right there at that well. The Scripture says that when it happened to her, she turned around and left her water pot and started running back toward town.

I want you to get this picture. A woman has just been saved. She is so excited, she doesn't know what to do. She starts running back toward town. The disciples had bought their groceries and were on their way back out to the well. Evidently, they must have passed each other again. This time, if the men hadn't stepped off the path, she would have run straight through them. I want you to get this point. Those disciples didn't talk to that woman when they were going into town and they didn't talk to her when they were coming back out from town. They just barely did remember that she was there.

The disciples got back to the well and were a little put out about the fact that Jesus had been talking to a *Samaritan* woman. At any rate, they finally said, "Here's supper, let's eat." Jesus said,

"I have already eaten." He added, "I have meat to eat that you don't know anything about." The disciples started looking at each other real funny. They thought Jesus had lost his mind.

Let's get back to the woman. After she passed these men and went back into town to the very store where the disciples had been buying groceries, she said to the men who had sold them the groceries, "Come, see a man which told me all that ever I did." Watch what happens. The entire community began to come out with the woman toward the well. She brought the whole grocery store with her and, while they were on their way out to the well, Jesus said, "Don't say four months and then come at the harvest." This tells us that this was not the harvest time. He continued, "Behold, . . . lift up your eyes, and look on the fields; for they are white already to harvest." What do you think Jesus was pointing to when he said this? I'll tell you what he was pointing to. He was looking at the entire city that this woman was bringing to him.

Boy, if that story doesn't hit the nail on the head, I don't know what does. Here was a group of disciples who were supposed to be witnessing for Jesus. They were supposed to be interested in helping people. Jesus had taught them that the most important thing they would do would be to reach people for him. And what were they interested in? Dinner!

Do you know why we don't win more people to Jesus? Because most of our churches are more interested in dinner than they are in helping people find Christ. Sometimes I'll get around a preacher and he'll start talking to me about his budget or his new building. Right there, I know he's not winning people to Christ.

I talked to a preacher recently and he said, "Boy, do we have problems." I said, "What are they?" He said, "We're $30,000 behind in our budget." I said, "Why don't you go out and win 300 people to Christ and teach them stewardship?" He looked at me like I was real strange and walked away.

I don't know how long it will take us to get it through our heads that churches don't have financial problems, they have spiritual problems. There isn't a problem that a church has that wouldn't be solved if everybody would start trying to bring people to Jesus. Most Christians I know are just like those disciples. We get all tied up in material things and, as a result, we begin to leave undone, week after week, the most important thing that we are supposed to do—bring people to Jesus. We keep passing people on the way back and forth to town. We keep passing unsaved people every day. We pass them coming and we pass them going. We don't speak to them about Jesus and we don't bring them to Jesus. We just go our way and keep taking care of the material things and all our own obligations.

Evelyn Linton in San Antonio

A few years ago I was in a crusade in San Antonio, Texas. In a crusade such as this, I always like to go to the local nightclubs or taverns to give a witness for Jesus in the evening after my local crusade has concluded. San Antonio, that year, the place where I was to go was the "Greengate Club," a strip joint of notoriety for the past 17 years. It was owned and operated by Guy and Evelyn Linton. It was located across from the Greyhound Bus Station downtown where every military man who came to San Antonio would frequent. They all knew about the go-go girls and the strippers that were always available to see at the famous Greengate Club.

On my first appearance there, I had arranged through a public relations man to go in and speak. On my next trip to San Antonio, I was invited by Evelyn Linton to come back and speak in her club, so I did. That night, I came to the time when I would conclude my remarks on the stage of the strip joint, surrounded by the strippers and a club full of curious people who wanted to see what a preacher would do in a setting like that. I asked Guy and Evelyn Linton to come forward and stand next to the stage and I had everyone bow their heads to pray. Some were laughing and some were cursing, and in the background, music was now being turned on. You could hear the glasses and bottles making their noise but I prayed for that couple and I coveted their lives that night for Jesus Christ.

They invited me to come to their home and stay, which I did. On Saturday afternoon, in their home, kneeling around their coffee table, I had the joy of winning this couple to faith in Jesus Christ. Evelyn Linton, a woman of notoriety in the city of San Antonio, had a news conference the next day with television cameras there, radio and newspaper reporters also there, said to the city of San Antonio, "I was instrumental in breaking the laws of this city so that strip-teasing could be legalized. I worked hard to bring strip-teasing into this city to help corrupt the morals of this city. I have asked God to forgive me through faith in Jesus Christ and he has forgiven me of my sins. Now, I want San Antonio, Texas, to forgive me. I want every mother to forgive me. I want every young lady and especially every strip-teaser I taught how to dance and strip, to forgive me."

Evelyn Linton, a woman whose reputation was not too well received by the social segment of the city, asked forgiveness of that city. This woman led many of these former dancers and strippers to the Lord. Many friends of the family were led to the Lord. Many of her neighbors and people who used to come in and see her at the club were led to the Lord. This is the story of a woman who, after her conversion, made me think so much of the Samaritan woman who took the same energy she had wasted and dedicated it unto God and became one of the most sought after speakers and soul-winners in the state of Texas. So I say, "God bless you, Evelyn, keep bringing them to Jesus Christ."

Ruth Grammer in Nashville

My heart is filled with joy when I think of the many women who have helped bring other people to Jesus Christ. I am sure you have heard of Billy Grammer of Nashville, Tennessee, the great outstanding Grand Ole Opry singer who had a gold record with a song called "Gotta Travel On." Billy used to tell how he would not have come to hear me preach if his wife had not insisted that he go to church with her. He asked her, "What church is he preaching in?" She replied, "It is not a church; it is the Nashville Municipal Auditorium. Many of your friends will be there and

many people who love country music will see you and it may even
help your image as a country music singer. I want you to go, honey."
So Billy Grammer went to see his son, Billy Grammer, Jr.

He said, "All right Billy, if I'm going, you're going too. So, let's
go."

That night the Grammer family came and heard me preach.
The Holy Spirit blessed the message as he always blesses the Word
of God, and Billy Grammer was brought under tremendous conviction. That night he was seated in one area with his wife and his
son was in another area with some of his friends. When the invitation was given, a few more verses were being sung and Billy
Grammer's heart was pounding away as the Holy Spirit convicted
him of his sins. He knew he needed what I was trying to get him
to do and that was to let the Lord come into his heart.

Billy had always pretended that he was a Christian. However,
when he came to the altar that night, he prayed a prayer that
I led all the others in—a prayer of faith accepting Jesus Christ
as Lord and Savior. When Billy Grammer raised his head, his
face looked so happy because he had let the Lord come into his
heart. He looked over to his left and there was his son, Billy, who
had also come to give his heart to Jesus and didn't even know
that his dad had come too. They immediately went to each other,
rejoicing in the Lord!

Here is an experience of a dad and a son saved, and now full-time
witnesses for the Lord. Billy Grammer is a lay speaker and his
son is singing in groups across the country, already dedicating
himself to the service of the Lord. Here is a family that is together
now in Christ because a woman brought her man to Jesus.

Joyce and a Drunk in New Orleans

When I was first converted, my wife was a little skeptical about
my sincerity. After a few weeks and months, she saw that my
experience was real and exciting to me. She started to want to
yield more of her life unto the Lord. There are many people who
are saved today because my wife led them to the Lord.

I remember those days of training and learning and sharing our testimony together. After television became one of our outreaches, my telephone became very popular at home. On a particular Sunday morning after our television show was played in New Orleans, a man called my home. My wife answered because I was out of town. A man who had been drinking was on the other end of the line. He told her how he enjoyed Bob Harrington on television. He told how he had sat there with a beer in his hand and watched Brother Bob preach about Bourbon Street. He kept talking almost endlessly. He didn't come right out and say he wanted to be saved. He didn't know how to say "saved" things. As Joyce listened to him, she thought at first, well, he's a drunk and doesn't know what he's doing!

Maybe the drunk didn't know what he was doing but the Holy Spirit did. Joyce kept listening and trying to encourage the man. She finally talked him into going to Sunday School with her at the First Baptist Church in New Orleans. This is the church where my wife has taught Sunday School and worked with young people for a long time now. She is presently the director of the Women's Missionary Union.

She said, "I'll pick up you and your wife and you can ride to Sunday School with me."

This is what it means to bring them to Jesus! Bringatation! Going and getting them. Sometimes people don't intend to carry out their promises because they really don't know what to do. They are lost, blind, dumb, and dead. They are past feeling and they need all the "bringing" they can get from someone who has a good case of bringatation!

My wife went by and picked up this couple and took them to Sunday School. They listened to the lessons and got under conviction and gave their hearts to Jesus Christ. A couple of men from our church followed up on this couple and got them to make a public confession of faith in Christ and join the church. This couple has since moved out of New Orleans but constantly call us and thank my wife for what she did. Here was a woman who brought a couple to Jesus.

Seminary Students Becoming Foreign Missionaries

A year after my conversion I wanted to go to the seminary and so I chose New Orleans Baptist Theological Seminary, which was near my home. I enrolled as a student. My wife and daughters came with me and we moved into one of the seminary apartments. I became concerned during some of our chapel services that I would see young people going forward to become foreign mission volunteers. Their plans were to become a missionary somewhere in a foreign land out in the future.

I wondered why I never did see these people witnessing and winning souls for the Lord. It amazed me when I kept seeing people who thought these who surrender to become foreign missionaries were really something special. The fact is that they are. It is a big decision to leave your family, your land, and those you love to go out and meet people you don't know and tell them about the Lord. That is a special group.

But the thought kept coming to me, "I wonder if it is going to be easier to witness in Africa than it is in Louisiana? Why are they not soul-winners while they are here at the seminary? Why don't they witness at the shopping center or downtown at the department stores where some of them work?"

Most of the ones I knew were simply professional students. Sometime I'd get concerned about the state of our foreign fields. I'd see administrators of hospitals that are there from America. I'd see teachers in schools that are there but still I did not see too many soul-winners. I believe you can hire hospital administrators and schoolteachers anywhere you desire. However, I think whenever a person surrenders to become a foreign missionary, he should first of all be a soul-winner.

This makes me think of the group that was with Jesus while he was dealing with the Samaritan woman and she was going back and forth to town bringing people to Jesus. These particular professional disciples were so busy being active that they forgot what they were being activated to be!

I think many of our students need to reevaluate their calling as a missionary, whether it is a home missionary or a foreign missionary. The greatest need in a foreign land is the same as it is in America—to bring people to Jesus.

The story of the fourth chapter of John is significant, not because it merely tells about a woman who brought people to Jesus. It really tells about a new Christian who was doing the right thing when all of the old Christians were doing the wrong thing. I think sometimes we get the idea that there is a seniority about the Christian life. I think we get the idea that all of the new Christians are supposed to be excited and on fire for God. I think we get the idea that witnessing is for a few people who still are excited about being Christians. The fact of the matter is that the call to bring people to Jesus, involves all of us. Thank God this Samaritan woman did the one thing she was supposed to do—bring people to Jesus. I hope she never stopped doing that.

I have a feeling that someday, when I get to heaven, I am going to see a very strange sight. There is going to be a bunch of disciples who will be embarrassed every time they pass a particular woman who will be there. Because everytime they pass her, there will be an entire army of people behind her. One of them is going to be the man who sold the disciples their groceries. He is going to be in heaven, but not because of the disciples. He is going to be there because a woman did the first and most important thing that she was supposed to do—bring people to Jesus.

3

It's All for Evangelism
—Or Is It?

Evangelism is the most important thing we do. Isn't it? No, it isn't! The most important thing we do is what we spend the most time doing and give the highest priority. That rules out evangelism.

In the early '60's, you will remember that a number of states were using the slogan, "It's All for Evangelism—Cooperative Program—It's All for Evangelism." This state made it perfectly clear that everything they did was really for evangelism.

After three years here was the result: the state showed gains in every area—more in Sunday School, more money, more in WMU, more leadership awards.

What about evangelism? During the three-year period, the churches baptized 1,000 less each year than the year before!

Everything gained but evangelism, and yet, it was all for evangelism!

As Christians, we are notorious for doing well in everything but the one thing we were called to do—win people to Jesus Christ.

Evangelism Is First with God

We better get something straight—evangelism is first with God and it better be with us.

Immediately after my conversion, I became a soul-winner automatically. I didn't know what a soul-winner was, but I became one anyway. It just seemed to be a natural expression for me to tell others what had happened to me when I met the Lord as my Savior. By the way, I haven't gotten over this first love yet and don't plan to.

I was encouraged to go to the seminary and there I got to enjoying the studies. The first thing I knew, I was enjoying my evangelism outreach more than my study inreach! I know that study is important but I knew by the way the teachers were talking and by the way I felt inside that I needed to learn more about how to study to show myself approved unto the Lord. Of course, sometimes study can become bad if you forget the good reason that you are studying.

I was called into the office of the president one day because everybody was concerned about the fact that I was absent too much from class. I was preaching so many revivals and getting so many people saved, that sometimes I would miss too many classes and began to make unsatisfactory grades.

I went in to see Dr. Leo Eddleman, who was, at that time, the president of the seminary. I can remember that, with good intentions, he made a recommendation to me. He talked with me about the fact that my wife wanted me to do the things that would be pleasing to God and get myself more qualified to be a better preacher or evangelist. She sat there and listened as the president made his recommendation. He said, "Bob, you should put a three- to four-year parentheses in your life and just withdraw from things to study and prepare and get yourself an earned doctorate of theology. You would be one of the few full-time evangelists around the country with an earned doctor's degree and you would really be qualified to be a better evangelist."

This sounded good. It really made my wife perk up. She could just hear the phrase, "Dr. Bob Harrington." A thought came to me and I shared it with as much love as I could to the president of the seminary and also with my wife. I told them that if I put my life in a parentheses for three or four years and left off evangelism, that when my years of parentheses were over, I would still be in that parentheses because I would have dedicated more to me than I had to the Lord. I told them that I thought it was a dangerous thing for any Christian to take a parentheses from soul-winning. So I told the president, "Thank you, but God didn't call me for that particular way of obtaining an education."

This is the reason that evangelism is first with me. Maybe I could sound a little more theological if I had a doctor's degree. But, you know, if I had to forsake evangelism for education, then I'd rather be an ignorant evangelist knowing less about some things and still be more evangelistic. I didn't want to be an evangelist who knew a lot and was not very evangelistic.

All during my growing up days in Sweet Water, Alabama football and sports were fascinating to me. These occupied much of my time and most of my thinking. After I went into the ministry, April 15, 1958, my motivation for sports was sidelined. I have since found out that my dedication to God has not only become my calling—my profession—but also has developed into my hobby.

Many times I am asked on an interview show what my hobby is. I have to pause and look at them with mixed emotions because they expect me to say, "Fishing, hunting, golfing, tennis, or sports of some type." But I look them straight in the face and say, "My hobby is evangelism. My hobby is spreading the good news that Jesus died for sinners. My hobby is soul-winning."

I know this sounds strange to people who hear it and even sometimes strange for a preacher to say it, but I must truthfully confess that this is my hobby. My hobby is witnessing for Jesus. I've tried golf, but I never could really get into it; so my golf bag is now in the closet at my home.

I tried tennis. I bought a tennis racket and got all the little outfits to wear. I played it a while and I would find myself out on the tennis courts witnessing to people about the Lord and my time would be up on the court and I would have to go back home.

Then I tried swimming. I have a pool nearby at my home and I thought this would be just the type of exercise I need. I guess, just to be honest, I have the most exciting time of witnessing and sharing my faith in Jesus Christ. I have found out that, thank God, my calling to preach has also become my hobby and that my hobby shall always be evangelism.

I recall the story of the lighthouse keeper. He had one job—to keep the light burning. He even had an emergency vat he could use in case the main vat ran out of fuel.

One day there was a knock at his door. A man in a motorboat was out of gas. The lighthouse keeper felt sorry for him. He took some fuel out of his emergency vat and gave it to the man.

The next day he had another caller. Someone else needed fuel. He had heard how kind and helpful the lighthouse keeper was.

The lighthouse keeper became the most popular man in the community. They made him president of the chamber of commerce. He became known as the most benevolent man in town. Everyone knew that if they had trouble and could make it to the lighthouse, they were in safe hands.

Late one night there was the sound from a ship in distress. The keeper awakened to see the light going out in the tower. He raced down the staircase and switched the turn-key to the emergency vat. It was empty! That night a ship crashed on the rocks at the foot of the lighthouse.

It made no difference that he had helped many people in lesser ways. The fact was that a ship crashed because he had failed to do the one thing he was there to do: keep a light reaching out into the darkness.

There are many things a Christian can do to help his fellowman. And there are endless little things a church can do for people. But there is only one thing that Christians have been called to do before all else and above all else: keep the light of the gospel reaching out to a world in the darkness of sin.

Evangelism is first with God and it better be with us.

Evangelism Is First with the Christian

You may be doubting what I have said up to this point. I can hear some of you saying, "It may be true that some Christians are supposed to witness but I think we all have different talents. It may be that God expects some of us to do the witnessing and others of us to do the other chores that need to take place around the church."

There is only one thing wrong with this line of thinking—it is a lie born of the devil! The devil would be the happiest man in hell if he could convince Christians that only some of them were supposed to witness. The next thing he would do is convince the ones who were witnessing that they were only supposed to do it part of the time. This is why Christianity is so weak today. We have listened to the devil instead of God for our commission and have ended up with a minority group of God's "half-witnesses."

Let me ask you a question: Why do you think God left you on this earth after he saved you? You are now his child and he isn't going to let you go. You now have a home in heaven, waiting for you. Why doesn't God go ahead and take you to heaven, since we all agree it is going to be better than what we have on this earth? I'll tell you why God has left you on this earth—for one reason and one reason only—to help take other people to heaven with you!

When I first surrendered to preach, I tried to get to the bottom of what makes some of the great men of God tick. Billy Graham said that he only wanted to be one thing—an effective soul-winner. Dwight L. Moody said that he only wanted to be one thing—an effective soul-winner. Therefore, that's what I decided I was going to be.

When I opened up my office on Bourbon Street, I got a number of reactions and all of them were bad. People in general thought I was after a fast buck and a loose woman. Other ministers thought I was a sensationalist. The folks on Bourbon Street thought I was a nut. I can tell you this—there are many on Bourbon Street who don't think that anymore.

I remember one nightclub owner on Bourbon Street early in my ministry. I will call him John. I went in his club one night but he wouldn't let me talk with him. He tried to run me out, but I ordered a Coke and paid for it. He had to let me stay. I tried to talk with him, but he would walk away.

Night after night I came to his club and ordered a Coke. Some of the girls, who didn't know who I was, started coming to the table to get me to buy them a drink. I would order a Coke, pull out my New Testament and start telling them about Jesus. One night, two of his strippers got saved and walked out. The nightclub owner called the police and tried to get me thrown out. They said that unless I was disturbing the peace, I had just as much right to stay as anyone.

Finally, one night, after a number of his girls had left, the nightclub owner came over to my table, sat down, and asked me a question. He looked at me with a scowl on his face and said, "Why do you keep coming here?" Without hesitation I responded, "Because Jesus sent me to you." That man is on his way to heaven today. And it isn't because I did anything so unusual. I simply did the one thing God called Christians to do—tell others the story of Jesus.

Evangelism Was First with Jesus

We are all familiar with the Great Commission that Jesus left us, "Go ye into all the world . . . and preach the gospel." Sometimes we forget that Jesus not only *said* that, but *did* it!

Jesus Christ had a three-year public ministry where he only did one thing. He spent his entire time trying to get people to transfer their membership from hell to heaven.

The reason people stopped following Jesus was because "evangelism" was all he did and it got more dangerous every day.

Whenever Jesus Christ preached, he could get 5,000 people to listen to him as long as he fed them! When Jesus cut the food and simply preached, only 500 showed up.

One day Jesus said, "I'm not going to preach, all I want you to do is come together and pray." Only 120 people showed up.

One day Jesus tried to recruit people who wouldn't hear a sermon but would simply go out in pairs and knock on doors. Only 70 showed up.

And one day Jesus put an ad in the local paper trying to recruit men who would let evangelism be a full-time job. Only twelve responded to the ad and even one of those was a reject.

One night Jesus said to the eleven he had left, "Gentlemen, tonight evangelism is going to get a little touchy. We are going to be witnessing to soldiers who will be trying to kill us." Only three of the eleven went with him that night.

Finally, Jesus said to the three, "This time our evangelism is going down a dead-end street. At the other end of it there's going to be a cross." Of the three, only one went with him—John.

Think of it—of the 5,000 who ate; and the 500 who listened; and the 120 who prayed; and the 70 who went; and the 11 who worked; and the three who dared; only *one* went with him all the way to the cross. And they ended up calling him John, the evangelist.

Was Jesus proud of John for making evangelism first? Well, you'll have to ask Jesus that. But I know this: on the cross, Jesus told John to take care of his mother. And John wrote the most important of the Four Gospels. And Jesus gave John the vision that we have as the last book of the Bible—the book of Revelation. And furthermore, when all of the others were dead—John, at the age of 100, was still telling the world about Jesus.

Conclusion

And before I close, I must add one word. Evangelism is not only first with God, you and Jesus, but it is also first with the unsaved man. Because you see, that man already has a reservation in hell today. And he can't change it until somebody tells him about Jesus.

I can't see how any Christian can justify the fact that he doesn't witness for Jesus Christ. I heard someone say recently that the word "saved" is simply a word that describes the process by which God turns a lost person into a soul-winner. We have all been saved to serve. And our service to God is to help bring people to heaven with us. There is no credential any Christian can have that is more important than that he tries to win people to Jesus Christ. I am convinced that God has called some to be evangelists and some to be teachers and some to be pastors. But I am also convinced that God has called all of us—young and old, rich and poor, brilliant and dumb—to try to help bring people to Jesus before it is too late. If you are not trying to win people to Jesus Christ, then nothing else you do is pleasing to God.

4

The Growth of a Witness

I remember during my first days of being saved how I wanted to grow so fast. I wanted to do so much. I wanted to tell everyone I met about Jesus. Immediately after my conversion, I began telling people about my experience with the Lord. I knew I needed to grow as a witness. I needed to learn more about the things of God.

I remember those first days as I struggled to be a witness. I would take the Bible in my hand. It would be difficult for me to find the right places in the Bible. I had trouble even pronouncing the words in the Bible. But it became alive to me. When some of my friends would show me certain verses, I would underscore them. Then I would put the page number in the Bible as a reference down at the border of my Bible.

Then, when I would be witnessing to someone on the street, or on an elevator, or in a car, or in a bar, or at a bus stop, or in an airplane—wherever I went, I was always witnessing—I would take my Bible out and talk to someone.

I would say, "Let's look together and find the way because I've only recently found the way myself and I'm not familiar with all of the things that you're supposed to do. Now, let's go. Here it says Romans 3:23." Then I would say, "Now, let's read it together because these words are so new and fresh to me. I may not pronounce the words properly, but I want you to see what God says and not just how Bob Harrington says it."

So we would look together at the Bible. We would see how that verse says, "All have sinned." I would say to the man, "This is you. This is me. This is everyone who has ever breathed a breath of God's kindness. All have sinned." Then I would say, "Now, let's look down here at the bottom of the page to see where we go next." The man would say, "It says page 70." So we would turn to page 70. It would be Romans, the sixth chapter and the twenty third verse which says, "The wages of sin is death, but the gift of God is eternal life through Jesus Christ our Lord."

Then we would go ahead and discuss the choice that would be there—the wages of sin being death or the gift of God being eternal life.

Then I would say in just as simple language as I know, "Which way do you want to go, man? Which route do you want to take? Do you want to pay the wages of your sins, or do you want Jesus to take those wages so you can have eternal life through Jesus Christ our Lord?" I found out in growing as a witness that the people that I witnessed to actually helped me grow as a witness.

I don't want to give the idea that becoming an effective witness for Christ is an easy thing. It's simple, but not necessarily easy. Many people fail to become a good witness for Christ because they get the cart before the horse. Let me explain what I mean.

There are three basic growth processes in the physical life. First, we come into the world being fed by someone else. A little baby would starve if somebody didn't feed him. Second, we move into a phase when we learn how to feed ourselves. We learn how to hold a knife and fork and put food in our mouths and chew and swallow it. Third, we move into a category when we start feeding others. We start earning money and raising children. Now, the simple truth is that a person is never going to be able to do a good job of feeding someone else until that person has learned how to feed himself.

These same three growth processes are true in a spiritual life. First, a new Christian is fed by others. He wouldn't know where to begin if someone didn't teach him the ABC's of the gospel. Second, a Christian learns how to feed himself. He learns how to study the Word of God. He learns how to develop a prayer life. Third, he reaches the place where he is ready to feed others. He is ready to bring other people to Jesus.

Many Christians fail at the job of trying to be a witness because they go from step number one to step number three. They go from being fed by others to feeding others. They fail to realize that the most essential factor of being an effective witness is learning how to depend upon the Spirit and power of God. You see, being a witness for Christ involves not only what you say to others, but what you are as a person. You can be a car salesman and also be a no-good rascal. It really will not affect how good you are at selling cars. But, you can't sell Christ to someone else unless you are a satisfied customer yourself.

Let me expand on these three growth processes and then I want to ask you a question.

Others Feed You

Before you can become a Christian, someone has to tell you about Jesus. After you become a Christian, someone has to show you where to go to find out certain basic facts about God and Christ and the Bible and life and death and eternity. The book of Hebrews compares this to feeding milk to a baby. This is why the Bible uses the phrase, "Being born again." No matter how old you are physically when you become a Christian, you become a babe in Christ. In your early spiritual development, you have to depend upon preachers and Sunday School teachers and interested Christian friends to help you grow as a Christian.

Feeding Yourself

There are many things you can do to feed yourself as a Christian.

1. *Evaluate.*—You can take a look at your life. There are certain things that must go and certain things that must stay.

2. *Regulate.*—A growing Christian needs to regulate his calendar. He needs to set aside definite times that he is going to use for

his own spiritual development. You will never have time for prayer unless you set a time for prayer. You will never have time to read your Bible unless you set a time to read your Bible.

3. *Select.*—A growing Christian ought to pick out other friends who are strong Christians. You ought to plan to be around them. You ought to watch what they do. You ought to draw strength from them.

4. *Secure.*—A growing Christian can get his hands on anything to read that will help him grow. You can read great books about other Christians. You can make a practice of filling your mind with anything that will help you grow as a Christian.

5. *Pick out a prayer mate.*—Every businessman ought to pick out another businessman to pray with at least once a week. Every woman ought to pick out another woman to pray with at least once a week. You should learn to help each other.

6. *Put aside time each day for meditation and prayer.*—We're living in a world that is hurrying; we're all running. We never do slow down, but a growing Christian has to slow down and wait on God.

Feeding Others

If you've done the above things, you are ready to tell other people about Jesus. You are ready to touch other lives. You are ready to be an effective witness for God. You are ready to feed others spiritually.

Now, I want to ask you a question. I want you to be very honest. Maybe you are saying that you haven't become an effective witness for Jesus Christ. Is it possible that you've gone from step 1 to step 3? Is it possible that you went from being fed by someone else to going out and trying to feed others? Is it possible that you've tried to become a witness for Christ before you really have learned to feed yourself spiritually?

Most Christians I know are still babies. They are still sitting in preaching services being fed by some preacher or a Sunday School teacher.

Every once in a while this person will get under conviction and go out and try to witness to someone for Christ. They fail. The reason is simple: They are trying to feed others and they haven't ever begun to feed themselves.

You see, this is a secret that can't be kept. Unsaved persons will be able to see it. If you are shallow, if you haven't learned how to feed yourself, if you haven't tried to grow as a Christian, they will be able to detect it. You will not have the spirit and power of God in what you're saying.

Do you recall Hans Christian Andersen's story of the king's existential garments? A group of weavers were going to make the king a robe that was going to be so beautiful that only the wise could see it. Of course, they weren't even going to make a robe. They were going to act like they were. However, the king wasn't going to admit that he wasn't wise. Therefore, they were able to pull off their scheme.

Finally, the robe was finished. The king was going to wear it in a parade. He took off all his clothes and put on the robe. Of course, the entire town had heard the story about the king's robe. Nobody in the town wanted to appear dumb.

Everyone was lined up in the streets as the king came by. People would say to each other, "Isn't that a beautiful robe? Doesn't the king have the most gorgeous looking new robe?"

Finally, the story says, that a "child of innocence" said, "Hey, the king doesn't have anything on!" For a moment, everyone was shocked and stunned into silence. Then someone said, "Did you hear what the kid said, he said the king doesn't have anything on." Soon someone else picked it up until finally, everyone was saying aloud, "The king doesn't have anything on, the king doesn't have anything on." You see, they weren't saying anything about the king, they were saying something about themselves.

This is what happens to a Christian who tries to feed someone else before he has learned how to feed himself. An unsaved person will say to himself, "This person is trying to clothe me and he's naked himself. This person is trying to feed me spiritually and he's starved himself."

If you have been guilty of trying to feed someone else before you've ever really tried to feed yourself, don't be discouraged. We have all been guilty of the same thing.

By all means, don't quit. Don't give up the job of trying to bring people to Jesus. Instead, have the guts to admit that you need to become a student of the Bible. Have the courage to admit that you need to spend more time in prayer. Take the time to grow as a Christian. And then, you'll be able to bring people to Jesus. And you won't have to face the embarrassing time when an unsaved person will say about you, "He doesn't have anything on."

Learn how to let unsaved people help you. If they bring up things you don't know, just tell them, "Hey, man, I'm kind of hung on that. I'll have to find out more and get back to you later." Don't ever pretend to be something that you're not. We are all just sinners saved by the grace of God, trying to help people out of the darkness and into the light.

People appreciate you when you are honest with them and when you're truthful with them. In fact, a lost soul needs to be led. Don't try to impress a person that you are so much sharper than he is because that makes him look dumb. Let them know that you once were lost but now you're found. That's an effective way to grow as a witness.

Let me come back to say that the most powerful weapon that a person can bring when he is witnessing to another person is the power of his own spiritual development.

Sometimes I may give the impression that the first thing that any Christian should do is go out and witness. This is not true. The first thing that we should do is get closer to the Lord ourselves. We should be filling our own spiritual reservoir with things that will strengthen us. We should be talking to other Christians, praying with other Christians, reading about other Christians, always looking for a way to grow spiritually.

I want to be an effective witness for Christ. Did you catch the fact that I didn't say I simply want to be a witness for Christ. I said I want to be an *effective* witness for Christ. A person will not become effective simply by knowing the right words to say. He will become effective by knowing the right relationship to have with Jesus Christ himself. We will be effective to the extent that we talk to God about men at the same time that we try to talk to men about God.

There is nothing more powerful as a tool for witnessing than for people to think that you are a good Christian yourself. I remember one time the story of a young boy named John Law, who was in a British school. Some of the boys in the school were trying to talk about religious things. One of them stopped and said, "Now, what is a Christian?" Someone answered, "John Law." That seemed to satisfy everyone because John Law was evidently the kind of young man whose life showed what it meant to be a Christian.

Later in this book I am going to talk in a much more practical way about how to go about talking to people about Jesus. Maybe some of the things that I will say at that time can help you. However, nothing I say will be able to help you as much as you will be able to help yourself. You must study the Word of God. You must spend time in prayer. You must read books by great Christian authors. You must fight the battle of temptation. You must become the kind of person that people will want to listen to.

Don't find yourself running from step 1 to step 3. Don't forget step 2. You must learn how to feed yourself. You must become a strong Christian. Then when you talk, others will want to hear what you have to say.

Anything that is not growing is dead. The greatest sign of life is growth. Therefore, unless you are a growing witness, you are a dead witness for Christ.

5

Bring Them to the Fire

Before you read this chapter, I want you to get your Bible and read the first two chapters of the book of Acts. There are some things there that have happened which are very important.

God called me to be . . . "An Evangelist." This is my single purpose in serving him. I feel the God-called evangelist is a gift to the local church. It is my God-given duty to help his church. My family and I attend our own church; not just Sunday morning but also Sunday night and midweek prayer service. My staff are all supporters of their local church program. We are tithers to our local church and have been since trusting Christ as our Savior and Lord. I was saved in a local church; baptized in a local church; called to be an evangelist in a local church; licensed to preach in a local church in Chickasaw, Alabama; ordained into the ministry in a local church in New Orleans, Louisiana; served as assistant pastor to Dr. J. D. Grey in New Orleans. Our two daughters are members and tithers in local churches in Waco, Texas.

Concerning doctrines: I am fundamental in my beliefs concerning God's Word but not fundamental in my attitude (meaning: I don't have my halo so tight that my horns protrude). I can disagree without becoming disagreeable. I have fellowship with all God's children even when we may differ over meanings, words, convictions, gifts of the Holy Ghost, and modes of church ordinances.

As long as Jesus Christ is our common denominator and our interest is in winning souls and making soul-winners out of the saved—I say: Praise the Lord . . .!

Now, let me say that I am for the church. I believe in the church. I am a member of a church. I attend Sunday School and prayer meeting every time I get a chance. But, I also know there is a time when it is a dangerous thing to bring an unsaved person, or even a new Christian to the wrong church. Maybe I should say it this way. Sometimes it's a dangerous thing to bring a new Christian to a church where the heat is turned off.

Sometimes we have the idea that the last command Jesus gave his disciples before he left the earth was to go. If you will read the fourth verse in the first chapter of Acts, you will see that Jesus cautioned his disciples not to go, but to wait. He told them not to go until they had received the power from the Holy Spirit. You see, these men were ready to go. They wanted to go. They were aching to get back to the people who had murdered Jesus and present them with the message that Jesus was alive. They wanted to say, "I told you so." They had the energy, but they didn't have the one thing that they needed most. As yet, they did not have the Spirit of God within their midst. They didn't have the broken heart, the concerned and passionate heart that God would need to use. So they waited.

When Jesus Christ ascended, these disciples didn't turn around and go back and begin to preach, they went back to a room and began to pray. They waited and prayed and waited and prayed for ten days and ten nights.

They didn't know they were going to wait ten days. The Lord didn't say, "Go pray ten days and then I will give you a blessing of power." I suppose it just took them ten days to get right with God. I suppose it took ten days for Simon Peter to admit that he had been self-centered.

I suppose it took that long for Thomas to admit that he had been a doubter. I suppose it took that long for them to get right and to get ready and to get broken so that they could be used of God and, finally, the power came.

When Pentecost came, there was no publicity. They didn't publish any advertisement; they didn't put up a billboard. They simply went out to the street corners as a group of happy, changed Spirit-filled Christians who were literally overflowing with the power and blessings of God.

In the twelfth verse of the second chapter it said, "And they were all amazed, and were in doubt, saying one to another, What meaneth this?" Question number one—remember that. That's the first question that they asked. What does this mean? In fact, these disciples were acting so happy, that in the next verse, "Others mocking said, These men are full of new wine." And so the people began gathering around saying, "What's going on here, what's happened to these men?" And as they got closer, Simon Peter began to tell them what had happened. He began to speak to them of Jesus Christ, of the death of Christ, of their sins, of the coming judgment, and of their need to be right with God. After they heard his message, they asked the second question in verse 37. "Now when they heard this, they were pricked in their heart and said unto Peter and to the rest of the apostles, Men and brethren, what shall we do?"

The first question, "What does it mean?" The second question, "What can I do to get it?"

Now, let me explain to you what I mean when I say that sometimes the most dangerous thing that you can do is bring a person to a church where the heat isn't on. When I think of a church, the word that comes to my mind is the word "incubator." You know what an incubator is. The interesting thing about an incubator is that it does not bring life; the machine merely sustains life. You'll find that an incubator in all of your hospitals is usually a very clean machine; very spotless and painted. But the way it is painted or how much glass it has—none of these things has to do with the function of the machine. So you see, the function of the machine is to sustain life, after it has been born, by warmth and by air.

You see, an incubator will not always sustain life. Sometimes it can kill a young baby. Suppose that a nurse has been negligent. Suppose she forgot to plug the machine into the electricity. When

the young baby was placed in the machine, it didn't have any
warmth. The beautiful paint meant nothing. The color of the
machine meant nothing, for the heat was off.

A church is like an incubator because nobody brings spiritual
life to an individual but God. You can't save a person. Only God
brings spiritual life into an individual, but God uses a church so
that when a person becomes a new Christian, he is placed within
a certain atmosphere conducive to growth. Through the interest
and compassion of surrounding Christians, and through the instruc-
tion of surrounding Christians, and through the dedication of
surrounding Christians, a new Christian or a weak Christian grows
within this environment.

God grows Christians the same way he grows bananas—in a
bunch. He places a newborn child of his within the atmosphere
of the church and within the warmth of the church. And the interest
and energy of these warm, dedicated Christians bring forth a
full-grown mature Christian.

But if the heat's off; if there is no warmth in the atmosphere
of a church; if there is no genuine interest for the new ones who
have come; if there is no one concerned about these young Christians—the same church that could have brought these young Christians to new life, will drive them away.

You see, the reason I call this a dangerous thing is because a
church doesn't automatically have heat. A church has to attain
it. Now, the important question is, "How do you get the heat on
in a church?" It's a very simple thing to get the heat on physically
in a church, but how do you get it on spiritually? How can we
be sure that the proper spiritual atmosphere is created in a church?

I read about a church in the east a little while back. Each year
they had a tradition that they would act out Pentecost, literally.
They would take away the pulpit furniture and would create the
scene of Pentecost and would literally act it out each year. They
had a way by which, at a certain climactic moment in the portrayal,
they would have fire dropped down to the altar. And, of course,
they had prepared for the fire below so that it wouldn't be dangerous.

One particular year a mistake was made and the drape of the baptistry caught fire and, as a result, the fire spread over the entire church and it burned to the ground. Later, a very caustic newspaper writer made the comment that as far as he was concerned, that was a pretty dangerous Pentecost!

You know, it might not be a bad approach. One day a preacher asked a friend if he had any ideas about how to get a good crowd at the church. The man responded, "Burn it down." Anytime you have a fire, you can always get a crowd. The man said it as a joke, but somehow I think this is what has to happen to a church. It has to get set on fire.

That's what happened to these men at Pentecost. Did you notice the progression of the questions a moment ago? Two questions were asked. The first question they asked as they came around saying, "What does this mean," and "What has happened to these men?" Then the second question was, "What can I do to have it happen to me?" Sometimes we forget the second question would never have been asked if it had not been for the first question. Many times we forget that no one is asking, "What can I do?" because they have not been asking of a particular church, "What's going on?" "What's happened here? What does it mean?" We get so highly organized in our churches that we forget that none of these things can substitute for the power of God.

So the question is, how does God start a fire in a church. One way he doesn't start it is by a majority vote. Many churches think they can settle any issue by a majority vote. That's simply not true. A church is not a democracy. A church is a theocracy. God is in charge of a church. Whenever a church starts to do anything, it ought to find out what the mind of God is.

A while back, a preacher said to me, "My church voted to have a revival." That's the most ridiculous thing I've ever heard. A church can't vote to have a revival. A church will have a revival when God starts a fire in that church.

You know how he starts a fire? God starts a fire in church the same way we learn to start a fire in the first place. God starts looking around in a group of people for one interested, concerned

Christian. He tries to find one man or one woman or one boy or girl—somebody who is interested in trying to win someone else. After he finds that one person, then he starts looking for one more. Then he rubs those two concerned Christians together until the sparks begin to fly from person to person.

This is how God has always begun revivals. This is how God has always begun great religious surges. God does not work through the enormity of a situation. He does not work through the tremendous mechanism of a church. God works through the intensity of a dedicated few who are willing to let their hearts be broken.

The only way a fire can get started in your church is through you, through your concern and through your compassion. That's the reason why it is so dangerous a thing to open the doors of a church and let hundreds of people come in where there is no heat. It would have been better for those people to drive to another town and find warmth than to come to a cold doorstep that has stained-glass windows.

One time I wrote a caption and I've tried to let it become the slogan for my own personal life. It said, "God, set me on fire and then call the multitudes out to watch me burn."

Bringing new people to Jesus is one thing; but after you bring them to Jesus, where are you going to find an incubator that will help them grow? Be sure you find a church where the heat is on. Bring them to the fire.

I have to admit, as an evangelist, that I can never send those who make decisions simply to the church of their choice unless it is a Bible-believing, witnessing church.

This raises the question about what a Bible-believing, Christ-honoring church is. You have a right to hear my answer on this. I think this is a church where Christ is exalted; where the Bible is believed and practiced; where the Holy Spirit is allowed to bring about conviction and you get people to come to the Lord; where people are being saved and filled with the Spirit of God; where a church is growing people to be witnesses for Christ.

People so many times think of a church as just being a building with a steeple and stained glass and a crowd of people inside.

The church is a local representation of the body of Christ who have assembled together to worship the Lord and Savior Jesus Christ. I have to insist that those who make decisions for Christ in our crusades across America will align themselves with a church that lifts up Jesus Christ as Savior and Lord.

One of the reasons that I go to some cities without any sponsorship at all is so that the churches who really care can surface and really get involved.

I did this in 1974 when I had a crusade in Nashville, Tennessee. Churches started calling and wanting to help. Pastors started calling and wanting to support the crusade. Johnny Cash and June Carter called and wanted to help out. Billy Grammer, from the Grand Ole Opry, called. Brenda Lee came and got involved in the crusade. Skeeter Davis called and came and got involved in the crusade. People in the high-steeple churches came. Many of the Jesus people actually dismissed their tent services in order to come be with us. This is the way I go in meetings across the country because this is where the fire really is.

There is no way that any evangelist can simply decide that he's going to have a revival and have the power of God there. We must pray, as Christians, until the fire falls from heaven. When the fire of God's Spirit falls, dedicated Christians will come out of the cracks in the wall in order to help the cause of Christ. This is how I am conducting my crusades today because I believe that we have been overly organized and sometimes we have actually put the fire out with too much of our own human preparation. I want God to set cities on fire and then call the unsaved out to watch them burn.

I want unsaved people to ask the question, "What is going on in that auditorium?" Then they will come and ask, "What can I do to be saved?"

6

Saved to Tell

When I think of Jonah, and Jonah going to Nineveh, I have to think of Bob going down to Bourbon Street. I think of Bob going to Vietnam; or Sunset Strip; or Las Vegas; or Greenwich Village; or dealing with the Mafia and all of the elements that the world seems to call so dark.

When I think of Jonah, I think of how God called me to go to the places where nobody else seemed to want to go—to all the dark places of the world—and to be a witness for Him.

When I first began shaping up my package and trying to decide what God wanted me to do, my wife was glad that I was a new man. But she didn't want me to be this kind of man. She didn't want me to be the kind of man that had to leave home. She didn't want me to leave home and go into areas that, as yet, seemed to be so untouched by Christ.

No witness for Christ had ever been established on Bourbon Street until that day when I went down there and opened up an office right in the middle of hell. I found me a spot to be located right next door to Al Hirt and down the street from Pete Fountain, right in the middle of the tourist area where people come to see the devil and all that he does.

Here the preacher goes, with a Bible in his hand and the Lord in his heart. I didn't take a whale to Bourbon Street; I took a streetcar. I remember the first day I went to Bourbon Street. I got on a streetcar because Dr. J. D. Grey sent me down there to try to locate a husband who had run away from his wife. While I was there, I felt led of God to establish a witness right there in the center of hell.

I remember how my wife said, "Alright, Honey, if this is what you feel you want to do and what God wants you to do, go right ahead."

Many times I'd get down there and I'd get discouraged. I'd look around that area and it was discouraging. I didn't try to put down people but people tried to put me down. They would let the air out of my tires. They would throw beer cans in my window. They would take my Bibles and destroy them. They would write dirty words on my door. They would draw obscene signs on the little window of my office where I didn't even have any furniture.

A little later, volunteer helpers started coming to help me witness. A little after that, I started a radio program that became quite effective. Then I would get down in a valley and I would say, "Oh Lord, am I doing any good? I think I'll find me a church."

I remember calling Dr. Wells, who was the associational missionary for New Orleans. I said, "Dr. Wells, I think I'm ready for a little church. If you find a little church somewhere with a parsonage next door, I believe I'll be ready."

He said, "Bob, God hasn't called you to pastor. You just stay in there where you are and let God continue to use you."

I said, "Well, Dr. Wells, you just keep me in mind." Because I felt, at that time, that it would be wonderful to go to a little church and not have the burden of Bourbon Street. It was lonely down there, far away from everything. Everybody was laughing at me. Christian people were ashamed of me.

But the Lord never left me. My dedication to him never wavered. I know how Jonah felt when God told him to do what he told him to do.

When we think about Jonah, we think about a rebel prophet of God. We think about the man who ran from God. Frankly, I think Jonah was one of the best prophets God ever had. Most

of the prophets in the Old Testament at least had the opportunity
to stay in their own land and with their own people, but God
asked Jonah to do a unique thing. He asked him to leave his home
and his people and to go into a strange land and tell those people
that they were loved of God.

God told Jonah to go to Nineveh. Nineveh was the capital of
Assyria. During the time of Jonah, Assyria was one of the most
brutal, military nations that ever existed. Some of the most atrocious
crimes that were ever committed by one people were committed
by the Assyrians. They were a feared and hated people.

You might say that Jonah, just like any of us, was saved for
a purpose. He was saved to tell other people that they were loved
of God.

In the first chapter of the book *Jonah was saved to tell and he
didn't*. But, keep this in mind; Jonah simply drew a line and said,
"I will tell my friends and loved ones that they are loved of God,
but I will not tell my enemies."

We would like to say that we are different from Jonah—that
we do not have any enemies as far as Christianity is concerned.
But, the fact is, most of us are not even willing to tell our friends
about Jesus.

Let me point you to a verse of Scripture in Ezekiel and then
ask you a question. "When I say unto the wicked, O wicked man,
thou shalt surely die; if thou dost not speak to warn the wicked
from his way, that wicked man shall die in his iniquity; but his
blood will I require at thine hand" (Ezek. 33:8).

Now let me ask you a question. Why do you think God left
you on this earth as a Christian? He did not leave you on this
earth to have vacations or to make money or to enjoy life. Your
home is in heaven. God left you on this earth for one reason—he
left you here to help bring other people to heaven with you.

That verse in Ezekiel means one thing. It means that someday
you and I are going to get to heaven and find out that there are
some people who did not make it to heaven and it was because
we failed to help tell them about the love of God. You might
say, "Well, I don't see how I can be happy in heaven if I know

that there are some people who didn't make it." You will be correct. It may take you a little time to get over the fact that you helped some people miss heaven. But, I can promise you this, you will get over it before those who miss heaven will get over it.

I am not saying that everyone who misses heaven will be your responsibility and mine, but you know the people for whom you are responsible. You know there are certain people that you see almost every day. You are the only link between them and God and you know that if you do not tell them of the love of God, no one will. I believe you and I are responsible for those people.

In the second chapter of Jonah *he was saved to tell and he couldn't.* In other words, Jonah refused to witness for God and God fixed him where he couldn't witness. He put him in the belly of a fish.

If you were honest, you would admit that there are some people that you do not witness to because you have spoiled your witness with these people. They are people who know you as you really are. They are people who have heard you take the Lord's name in vain. They are people who have seen you live a life that is unpleasing to God and the reason you do not witness to them is because your life has closed your lips.

In the third chapter of Jonah, *he was saved to tell and he did.* The Bible says that when Jonah got out of the fish, he made a three-day trip in one. He went to Nineveh and did what God told him to do in the first place. He told them of the love of God. He told them that they needed to repent and turn to God. And the Bible says that the entire city—120,000 people—repented in one day.

It is unfortunate that most of the time it takes God longer to get one of us right with him than it takes him to win an entire city.

The word "repentence" is very important in the book of Jonah. At one point it says that Jonah repented. And then later it says that Nineveh repented. And, finally it says that God repented. God literally changed his mind about the sinners of Nineveh. You see, God is always ready to change his mind about sinners. God is not willing that any man should perish. God is waiting on

Christians to repent and get right and go try to bring people to
him. And when we do, he will change his mind and also change
the reservations of other people from hell to heaven.

Every Christian has to decide for himself where his responsibility
will be. I do not believe, for instance, that I will ever have the
blood of New Orleans on my hands. I have preached to that city
more than any other preacher has ever preached to that city. My
television program goes in there every week. I have given it my
best. I think I can say the same thing about Los Angeles. I think
I can say the same thing about most of the United States. The
reason I bought my bus is because right now I want to drive back
and forth across the United States until every person who wants
to hear Bob Harrington talk about Jesus will have the opportunity
to hear Brother Bob.

And I want you to know that I don't ever plan to let my ministry
get into the situation where I am saved to tell about Jesus but
I can't. One of the saddest days of my life was the time I had
to dismiss a staff member because he forgot that his influence
was important. He got himself into a position where he could not
witness for Jesus Christ. No matter how I loved him, and no matter
how talented I thought he was, I had to let him go.

God called us to witness and that's what we're going to do. Let's
don't ever give up that task. Of course, there will be discouraging
times. If you read the fourth chapter of Jonah, you will see that,
even after that great experience that he had, Jonah still got discouraged. He questioned himself. He wanted to quit. I think God added
that little fourth chapter to the book to let us know that we should
never get discouraged. He was sitting out there and the sun was
beating down on him in his discouragement. And God came and
brought him some shade. My dear Christian friends, if we'll just
do what we're supposed to do, God will never let us down. God
wants to see us witness for him. And he wants other people to
be saved. And he wants to change his mind and take people to
heaven instead of hell. Let's do the thing we're supposed to do,
as Christians—bring people to Jesus.

7

The One That Got Away

In the tenth chapter of Mark there is a very interesting story. We have been talking about bringing people to Jesus. We are about to look at the story of a man who was not brought to Jesus. He came to Jesus under his own steam. It appears that he had everything to offer Jesus. But Jesus let him get away.

We have a lot to learn about witnessing by watching what Jesus does with the rich young ruler.

The rich young ruler was a very interesting individual. He was a young man who took the initiative to come and find out about religion. Very seldom does a preacher have a situation where an individual takes the initiative and seeks him out for help. This young man came running to Jesus. Not only that, he came in a sense of humility because the Scripture says that "he knelt down before Christ."

Keep in mind that this young man was a member of the Pharisees. He was religious to a degree. He was also a very wealthy man, and yet, he came in a sense of humility.

Strangely enough, he appeared to ask Jesus the right question. He said, "What can I do to inherit eternal life?" Now understand, this man already believed in life after death. He was a Pharisee. The Pharisees were committed to a belief in life after death. So this man already believed that life was going to go on forever, but the kind of life was what was bothering him because this man had found a life that seemed to be meaningless. It was a life that didn't have any real purpose to it and it was a life that he just wasn't looking forward to living forever.

I am always finding people who are trying to find out a good definition for hell. They want to find something that won't have fire in it. In other words, they want to find something that won't be really bad.

I'll give you a good definition of hell. Hell could be just nothing more than the extension for eternity of the predicament that you have already gotten yourself trapped into in this life. And don't think I'm watering down hell. Hell is everything the Bible says it is. Hell is a lake of fire that burneth and is not quenched. Hell is a place of darkness. Hell is a place where people cry out in anguish. Hell is a place where people remember forever and forever the things they should have done. Hell is a place of ashes. Hell is a place of loneliness. Hell is a place of emptiness. Hell is a place of separation. Hell is a great gulf where men will never be able to cross from darkness to light. But most of all, hell is the absence of eternal life.

This was the thing that concerned this man. His life had no quality to it. His life had no depth to it. It had no breadth to it. He came to Jesus and asked what he could do to get real life right now.

Watch how Jesus dealt with him. Most of us would call this young man a good prospect.

I've seen the days in my own ministry when I would probably have put that rich young ruler on my board of directors. I might have even put him as a trustee. I'm sure our Baptist seminaries could have found a place for him on the development board. When a man has the kind of credentials that this young man has, we don't necessarily want him to repent under today's standards. But Jesus did. Jesus wanted his heart.

If most of us had a rich young man come down the aisle in one of our services and offer himself, we would take him with no questions asked. But do you know what Jesus did? Here comes a young man running down the street; he kneels down before Jesus and asks about eternal life. He even says, "Good Master."

But Jesus responds and asks, "Why do you call me good? There is none good except God alone."

Jesus always had a way of getting behind the words that a person was saying, to the meaning of those words.

Jesus responded to the man's question about eternal life by saying, "Keep the commandments." And then he listed five of the last six commandments and he intentionally avoided the last one—covetousness. He didn't mention it. He said, "Don't murder; don't steal; don't lie; don't bear false witness; don't commit adutery."

Have you ever noticed that life isn't as complex as we think it is? Most people do not have a lot of problems. Most people just have one big problem. It is not always the same problem. With some people it will be something moral. With others it will be something academic. With others it will be something economic. But, usually there is one area where the person is being defeated day after day in his life and all of the rest of his problems are hiding behind that one big problem. And the day that an individual can get victory in that one area, he is on his way to total victory.

Jesus knew that about this young man. He listed all of the things that the young man was not guilty of. The man responded by saying, "Why, I have kept all of those things since I was a boy. I am not guilty."

Then, Jesus said, "All right, do this." And then he named six things. He said, "Go. Sell all you have. Give it to the poor. Come. Take up the cross. Follow me."

Jesus was not telling this young man that the only way to become a Christian was to become poor. He knew that this young man's problem was covetousness. He knew that money was his one big problem. Jesus was simply saying, "You go and straighten out the one wrong relationship in your life and come take up your cross and follow me." Jesus was, in essence, telling the young man to go get rid of the one thing that was standing between him and God and then he would be all right.

These were hard words to a young man of wealth. They touched him where it hurt the most.

Jesus wasn't trying to make it difficult on the young man. He just knew that if he let the young man in without solving his main problem, he would end up with a half-hearted follower who had his fingers crossed.

The Scripture says that the young man turned and walked away and Jesus let him go. This was the best prospect that ever came to Jesus and Jesus let him go.

Why didn't Jesus go after him? Why didn't he try to argue with the young man and get him to change his mind? I'll tell you why. Because, in the life of every individual there comes a time when that individual knows what God wants; when that individual knows what his response to God must be. And when that time comes, a man has to make up his own mind. It has to be his own decision. And even the Son of God, who came to this earth that men might live, had to stand there and let that young man walk away.

I wonder what happened to the young man. We do not know. We can only speculate. I can see the young man going home and talking to his wife about meeting Jesus. I can hear him say, "Boy, today I almost did a stupid thing. I almost sold the farm. I almost came to the place where I was going to take all of the profit and give it to the poor and follow this man Jesus Christ."

Or, the story could have ended another way. One artist painted the picture of this young man as turning away with a heavy heart; with his shoulders slumping; with his hands hanging to his sides in death and his feet dragging the ground. I can see this young man going home and sitting down to supper in silence. Finally, he speaks to his wife, "Darling, this home means a lot to you, doesn't it? Well, I'll tell you what I'm going to do. I'm going to sell it. I'm going to sell all my property and I'm going to follow Jesus." I can see the young man getting up the next day and going out to find Jesus to tell him that he was going to follow him.

We don't know how this story ends. But let me tell you something. I can tell you exactly how it is going to end for you. Because, you see, there are many of you reading this story who know what

God wants of you. You know those things in your life that are standing between you and a real spiritual commitment and you know what your response to Jesus Christ ought to be. You know what repentance would mean in terms of renouncing a life of self-seeking and receiving a life of power through Jesus Christ. Yet some of you are reading this and I have a suspicion that you are prepared to do the same thing this young man did—turn away from Jesus.

Let me tell you this: The saddest day in the life of any man is when he knows what God wants him to do and yet turns away from Jesus.

We have dealt with two things in this story—a man's heart and a man's treasure. Jesus never wants a man's treasure without his heart. Jesus knows that if a man puts his treasure in the right place, his heart will be there also. Jesus went straight to this man's treasure. He told him to give it away and come follow him.

When I witness to a man, I never do make it easy for him. I let him know that following Jesus is going to cost him everything he has. After awhile, I let him know that God is going to give him everything he needs. But I don't believe in letting a man off the hook. Following Jesus means doing it the way Jesus wants it done.

If a man doesn't want to follow Jesus, he can always go to hell. There won't be one person in hell who wanted to follow Jesus. There won't be a person in the darkness who wanted the light. There won't be a person down there who wanted to go up there. There won't be a person who suffers throughout all eternity who wanted to know Jesus forever. There won't be a person who spends eternity without the church who wanted to go to church and find Christ. There will not be a person who spends eternity without the Holy Spirit who wanted to listen to the Holy Spirit while he was alive.

I heard a man one time comment that while Jesus was in the grave, the devil said, "If he stays dead, we'd better thank hell because if he comes back to life, all heaven is going to break loose."

I don't know what happened to that rich young man. But I know that if he didn't accept Jesus, all hell broke loose for him. And I know that if he did accept Jesus, all heaven broke loose for him. That's the choice that every person faces—the difference between day and night; the difference between darkness and light; the difference between heaven and hell; the difference between life and death. I hope that he didn't get away forever. I hope and pray that no man that I ever talk to will get away from Jesus.

8

Others Who Got Away

I wish I could report that every witness that I ever made was positively accepted. I'd like to be able to say that everyone that I ever witnessed to responded positively and repented and asked the Lord to come into their heart and life.

I cannot say that. For every one that I witnessed to, and won, there are hundreds that got away. There are hundreds who say no to the Lord. I can think of hundreds where I led the husband to the Lord but the wife was not ready and didn't even want to come to Jesus. I can think of situations where the wife even left the husband because he became a Christian.

I can think of people on my staff that I led to the Lord. But one came and the wife or husband did not come. And in a situation like that, the Lord becomes a divider. There are many who have gotten away.

I have tried to spend my life rescuing the perishing and caring for the dying. Just because someone said no does not mean that we are supposed to give up on them. One of the attributes that I am trying to develop is persistence in my witnessing. Once I begin with a person, I am trying not to ever give up on that person.

I learned a long time ago that effective witnessing is sharing the power of God with other people and leaving the results to God. God did not call us to get results. He does not keep score of the ones who got away.

In the last chapter we discussed a young man who got away
from Jesus. I want to continue with the theme of those who heard
Jesus preach and yet didn't accept Him. I think it might be an
encouragement to some of us who try to witness for Christ to realize
that even Jesus lost some who came to him.

The sixth chapter of John is a very dramatic chapter because
it starts on a positive note and ends in a completely different way.
It starts with 5,000 people gathered around Jesus Christ to hear
him preach. There is a very human thing about the preaching
of Jesus Christ. Most of the time that he drew his largest crowds,
it was because he offered the people a free meal. In the sixth
chapter of John, he begins by offering people something to eat.
Thousands of people were willing to accept this, but as his sermon
continued, Jesus talked about sacrifice and the idea of death. He
began to talk about people eating his flesh and drinking his blood.
In the sixty sixth verse it finally says that the 5,000 people gradually
turned away and only a handful of people remained. What was
it that happened? The truth is that these people listened to the
message of Jesus and found that he was preaching about sacrifice
in terms of following him and they decided that following Jesus
was simply too hard. He told them that if they followed him it
would mean sacrifice and suffering and death and many of them
decided that this was simply too hard.

Martha Was Too Busy

In the tenth chapter of Luke, there is the story of a woman
named Martha who one day had to give an answer to the question
of why it was so hard for her to follow Jesus Christ. She said
simply that she was too busy. You remember the story. Martha
was rushing around with a lot of things going on. She was simply
too busy.

Many times people use this excuse with me as to why they fail
to witness for Jesus Christ. They simply say they are too busy.

Many times I try to get men to let go of some of their responsibilities and witness during a crusade. They very carefully tell me

that they are simply too busy do to it. The only problem with this kind of an excuse is that I learned a long time ago that a person is never too busy to do the things that he wants to do. Someday God is going to decide whether the things we wanted to do were as important as the things he wanted us to do.

The Rich Young Ruler Said Jesus Asked Too Much

In the last chapter, we discussed the rich young ruler. He found it hard to follow Jesus because Jesus asked too much. He was willing to give Jesus a little. But, Jesus didn't want a little from the man. He wanted everything. There are a lot of us who are content to give Jesus a little. I heard a preacher one time preach on the subject "Busy man, you have had a little day." You see, the secret of Christianity is that you haven't given God anything until you have given God everything. No one can out-give God. But God is never going to let a man follow him with a half-commitment.

John Mark Said Jesus Wanted Him to Go Too Far

Mark decided following Jesus was too hard because Jesus wanted him to go too far. Mark thought it would be fun following Jesus. He thought he was willing to do anything. One day God called him to go to a foreign country to preach. Mark got homesick and wanted to come home.

Every year I travel hundreds of thousands of miles to serve Jesus. I never think of going too far for Jesus. The only thing that is important to me is to be in the center of God's will. I honestly would rather be a thousand miles from home and in the center of God's will than to be in the center of my own personal pleasures and be a thousand miles from God's will.

As Christian witnesses, we have to face the fact that most people who hear about Jesus do not accept him. Most people turn away. Those 5,000 people in the sixth chapter of John turned away from Jesus. But they turned away from him before they had tried his way. But Jesus turned to the handful that were left, who had already tried him, and said, "Are you going to turn away, too?"

They said, "No, Lord, because we know that there's nowhere else to turn for thou hast the words of life."

Somewhere out there those 5,000 people who turned away from Jesus are going to find out that life is one long process of restlessness until they find their rest in God. God made every man in his own image. That means that he made a man to live for God. And, when a man does not live for God, he can never be at home with his own heart. And when a person truly tries Jesus Christ, he will not say that he was too busy or that it was too hard or that Jesus asked too much. He will simply say that he is sorry that he waited so long to come to Jesus.

Before I became a Christian, I was a salesman. I found that there were a lot of bad salesmen who lacked the ability to stop working with a person who kept saying no. I once had an insurance salesman tell me that a good salesman could not dwell too long on the ones who said no. He told me that you could ruin yourself as a salesman if you kept trying to win the person who refused to be won.

As a preacher, I have found this to be true. My heart almost breaks sometimes when people turn away. I find myself wanting to go back and try again and again to help people who refuse to be helped. But there are so many people out there who need the Lord. Our job is to keep on sharing the witness for Christ. There are some people who will never be brought to Jesus. There are some people who will never be helped. But there are millions of people who are simply waiting for the slightest indication that someone cares about them. We must take the story of Jesus to those people. We must keep witnessing to people everywhere they are, knowing that God will keep the score.

9

Who Needs to Be
Brought to Jesus?

I have mentioned earlier my experience after my conversion in
going to New Orleans and setting up a shop down on Bourbon
Street. You might say that I began my ministry in the area that
Billy Graham has described as "the middle of hell."

Much of the negative reaction that I received was from the
organized church people—the so-called "Holy establishment." They
would say that this is not the place for a man of God. They would
say it was like casting pearls before swine.

I remember one time that a group of ladies were touring the
city of New Orleans and sort of eavesdropped on Bourbon Street
to see what it was like. Upon returning to their home in the state
of Virginia, they wrote me a letter. I'm sure that they had good
intentions. They even indicated that they were writing after much
prayer. They said in full, "We are writing you this letter after much
prayer, feeling that God wants us to let you know that it isn't
right for you, a minister of God, to be down there on Bourbon
Street. We definitely feel that it is like casting pearls before swine.
We urge you to get out of the Sodom and Gomorrah area. We
urge you to get out of the area of darkness without God. We feel
that as long as you continue to stay down there, you are as guilty
as the people around you."

I could not help but think of the crowd that accused Jesus of

being a glutton and a wine bibber because he refused to identify
with the sin but he did identify with the sinners.

We need to realize that Jesus came to seek and to save those
that are lost. Everyone is lost until they are saved. And every person
who breathes the breath of kindness from God needs to be saved.

One of the principal things I have found out through my ministry
is that people do not easily and naturally come to the established
building of the church. Jesus told us who love him to go to those
who do not love him because he loves them. This is exactly what
I endeavor to do in my witnessing for the Lord wherever I might
be.

If we can accept the Scriptures, and I do, then we must believe
that Jesus did attend a lot of wild parties. He attended a lot of
banquets where the church crowd was absent.

I hope you understand the way I say this, but I can certainly
appreciate the problem that Jesus had. A lot of important men
heard about Jesus. They didn't want to come to his preaching
service. So instead, they invited him to their banquets. Naturally,
there was going to be a lot of drinking going on at these banquets,
but Jesus went anyway.

Now Jesus was not a drunkard. But he went to places where
there were a lot of wild things going on and he left himself open
to the charge by the simple process of association.

Why did he go to these places? The answer is so simple that
I hate to say it. He went because that's where the sinners were.
Jesus gave a very simple explanation. He said, "They that are well
have no need of a physician, but they that are sick. I came not
to call the righteous, but sinners to repentance."

The enemies of Jesus Christ—and strangely enough, these enemies
were related to established church—made two mistakes about Jesus.

1. They made the mistake of thinking that the church was *for*
the church.

Many of these "religious people" felt that Jesus owed his time
to those who already loved God. Many times people say to me,
"Bob, why don't you spend more time in the churches and less
time down there with those wild sinners?"

The reason why a lot of Christians don't bring other people to Jesus is because they have the mistaken idea that the only task that Christians have is to look out for other Christians. This is why most churches are dying. Most churches are content to make sure that they remember their member's birthdays, marriages, and funerals. They forget that the church is not for the church. The church is supposed to be an arena where people are brought to Jesus.

Whenever a church thinks only of itself and its own people, it is close to death. Whenever a group of Christians simply spends its time having little study groups and group therapy meetings, it is neglecting the one thing that it is supposed to do—bring people to Jesus.

I remember when I visited hospitals a lot. I came to see very clearly the meaning of what is called, "The circle of death." There is something that happens to a person who comes to the hospital who is a terminal case. I have watched people who come to the hospital and only have several months to live. You would not be able to know this by the way they looked or acted as they first came to the hospital. Many times a man would bring part of his office work with him. He would want to be sure that there was a telephone in the room. He would want the daily newspapers brought in. He would want a radio going and television. He would want to see all of his friends. He would talk to his secretary several times a day.

But as the weeks went by and the man began to get weaker from the disease that was eating away his body, he would gradually narrow his circle of interests. He would drop the calls from the office. He got to the place where he cared less about what was going on in the world. Mainly, he wanted his friends and loved ones to be around him every day.

Then the day would come when the man would stop reading the newspaper. He would stop watching television. He would be so weak that he would only care to have the very closest of his friends and loved ones around him.

Finally the time would come when the man cared to see no

one except the two or three loved ones. And then one day, the man would be in a coma and could not even honor them.

As I watched that death process so many times, I thought about the church. I thought about churches that I would consider to be alive and how part of their "liveness" had to do with the fact that they were interested in what was going on for Christ all over the world. They were interested in people who needed Christ in every part of the town—the rich, the poor, the young, the old.

And then I thought about some of the churches that appeared to me to be dying. I began to notice that they cared less for those people outside their ranks and spent most of their time taking care of each other on the inside.

I guess you might say that when a church reaches the place where it's only interested in honoring its own members' birthdays, marriages, and deaths and has stopped reaching out to win people to Jesus Christ, that church is close to death.

2. The second mistake that the enemies of Jesus made about him was thinking that the church was *at* the church.

When I first went on television, I used a bar for my pulpit. I received a lot of criticism about this. Some people felt that I should have a pulpit and the setting should be that of a church. But I don't go along with this because I have the conviction that most of God's work today is not being done in God's house.

I have the strong feeling that just exactly the opposite is true. Jesus said that he had to leave the Temple in order to go out where the people were. He talked about going into the highways and the hedges.

Most churches are weak because they spend all week getting ready for Sunday. We ought to be doing just exactly the opposite. We should be spending Sunday getting ready to go out and spend the week bringing people to Jesus.

You see, we can't get the world into our churches. If tomorrow everybody in the world decided to go to church, there wouldn't be enough room for everybody to sit down. But we can get our churches into the world. We can go out and try to bring people—not to church—but to Jesus.

Sometimes I think we ought to put a quarantine sign on the door of our churches. We ought to say on the sign, "Everybody inside has a disease. No one should go out and no one new should come in or the disease might get out of control."

Today we have to stop thinking about merely bringing people to church. We must think instead about bringing people to Jesus.

I have a minister friend who was preaching one time in Brazil in the city of Belem. On Saturday night he was going to preach a rally for thousands of people. That afternoon he had a very strange experience.

A truck pulled up on a vacant lot beside the building where the rally was going to be. It was not really a large truck, but there were eighty-eight people inside of it. These eighty-eight people were the entire membership of one little church that was two hundred miles out in the jungles of Brazil.

They had spent twelve hours coming through the jungle in that truck. They had come for one reason: one of the members of the church had a brother in Belem who was not a Christian. They had driven into the city to pick up that brother and bring him over to the crusade.

That evening, those eighty-eight people sat around that one man while he heard the story of Jesus. At the invitation, dozens of them walked with the man and brought him to the altar. He was saved. It was a beautiful sight.

Immediately after the service, those eighty-eight people climbed back into the old truck and started back out into the jungle.

That's what it means to bring someone to Jesus. That's what a church is supposed to be. How long do you think it would have been before that one unsaved man would have driven twelve hours out into the jungle to attend a church service? But that church did what they were supposed to do. They paid the price to bring one man to Jesus.

Why did Jesus Christ leave the Temple and go into the highways and hedges?

The answer is simple: because he was a friend of sinners. I say, thank God, because that's how I was saved—because Jesus Christ was a friend of sinners and Bob Harrington is a sinner.

If you will permit me an analogy between myself and Jesus, I think that one thing that is evident in my ministry is that I have a way of attracting sinners to me but repelling the self-righteous. I have found myself saying sometimes, if I could only get the Christian people pulling for me instead of criticising me, everything would be all right. But on the other hand, I would hate to think that old, dirty, low-down sinners would stop wanting to be around me.

I have learned that a Christian has to keep his eye on those people who need Jesus and go ahead and do his dead-level best to reach them for Christ. You can't listen to what some of the self-righteous people around you would say. I recall last year, speaking one evening at a church in Los Angeles. It was not a normal church service. It was a regional convention of the National Religious Broadcasters. At the end of what I had to say that evening, I gave an invitation. Many of the broadcasters and some of the other people were offended at the fact that I would dare give an invitation at their little convention. Therefore, a number of them began to leave while I was giving the invitation. So many were leaving that they crowded the aisles and were prohibiting other people from coming forward at the invitation.

I can't tell you how mad this made me. As strong as I knew how, I began to tell those people leaving to stop doing it. I told them that if they had one ounce of Christian blood in their veins, they would stop going away from that service while we were trying to bring people to Jesus Christ.

The next week, a psychiatrist who had been there that evening, wrote a letter to one of the officials of the convention and said, "My psychiatrist friend and I have been exploring Bob Harrington's behavior the other night and have come to the firm conclusion that the reason he lashed out at all of us at the end there, was because his mind has been completely demented by alcohol."

I do not know who that psychiatrist is and I'm glad I don't. I do not have time to fight off the temptation to get on a plane and fly across America and let him know what I really think about him. The thing that really shocked me was that the man wasn't willing to stop by saying Bob Harrington didn't have a right to scold us who wanted to leave. He had to proceed and give his scientific conclusion that my brain was saturated by alcohol. When I first heard this, I was completely flabbergasted. I tried to fathom why a man, who claimed to love God, would want to try to make such a ridiculous accusation against a preacher he didn't even know personally.

A few days later, another letter came across my desk. It was from a person who was having an alcohol problem. This individual happened to have been at that banquet that evening in Los Angeles where I spoke. He was one of the persons who fought his way past those leaving and came to give his heart to Jesus Christ. He was writing to thank me for giving that invitation.

I'm glad I can call myself a friend of sinners because that means I can call myself a friend of that man who came forward that night in that invitation. But you see, it means I can also call myself a friend of that psychiatrist who wrote the lying accusations about me because, whether he wants to admit it or not, he is a sinner too.

10

A Past That Will Not Die vs.
A Future That Will Not Wait

This chapter is going to be what you might call a "controversial" chapter. This is going to be true because I am going to use some words that usually are "danger words" for many Christians. But I am going to do it anyway because I feel that we cannot afford to let secondary issues keep us from the main task of bringing people to Jesus.

I am convinced that many of us are not bringing more people to Jesus because we are torn between two things: a past that will not die and a future that will not wait.

Change is the biggest story of 1974. I would not know where to begin to define all of the areas in which this change is taking place. Advertising has brought it on as the advertisement world crams down our throat things we don't really need while two thirds of the world still goes without.

Our own affluence that we are now enjoying helps feed advertising and adds to the change as past luxuries have now become present necessities.

The computer has brought on an era of change. It has impersonalized us and we don't like it.

In school we are a card. On the telephone, we are a circle digit. In the mail, we are a ZIP code. In the business world, we are a number. In sales meetings, we are a statistic.

Bob preaching on the runway of the original TV set for *The Chaplain of Bourbon Street*, national syndicated TV ministry

Brother Bob and Tiny Tim exchanging records in West Virginia

Young and old—men, women, and children—meet Brother
Bob in Raleigh, North Carolina

Brother Bob with Governor West of South Carolina (center) and Rev. Lonnie Shull, local chairman of the Spiritual Bowl

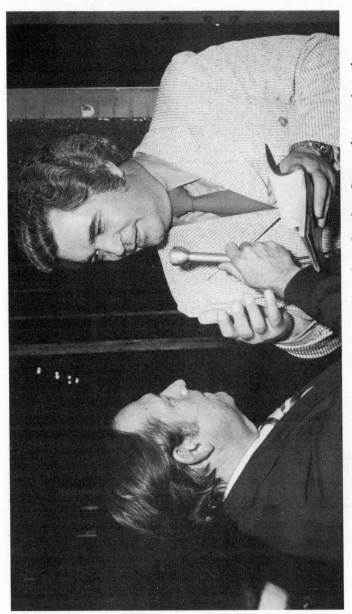

"The Chaplain of Bourbon Street" being interviewed on Bourbon Street—the occasion: the dedication of his chimes that ring out a song of faith each hour

Brother Bob and Nashville disc jockey Jim Black during a
recent crusade

John McDonald, famous Hollywood stunt man, was reached by Bob's preaching and writing.

Bob carrying the message where men are—here in Charleston, S. C.

This "double-exposure" picture symbolizes Bob's multi-ministries which reach out and BRING THEM IN!

Bob at a press conference in Garland, Texas—Bob uses all of the media to BRING THEM IN!

Bob believes in preaching the gospel to everybody everywhere—here he proclaims the Word in a Texas night club

During his Las Vegas Crusade 25,000 people responded to the BRING THEM IN! invitation. Find the misspelling on the sign.

Migration has added to this change. Do you realize that hundreds of thousands of people in America every year change their residence—move from one community to another?

We live in a day of the population explosion. Everywhere on earth births are increasing and death is being postponed. This means more people—all kinds of people.

We are living in a day of science where every single week, two hundred new words are added to the scientific dictionary.

Did you ever stop to think about how the single invention of the automobile changed so many things in America? It changed the layout of cities. It changed the kinds of jobs that would be available to a man. It changed the dating habits of young people.

All of these changes have piled in upon us and have created a new kind of world. It has caused us anxiety because we really don't know how to cope with it. Change always forces decisions.

The main question that concerns us is: how does this world of change affect a Christian? Today Christians are divided and I don't mean between Catholics and Protestants. Rather, today the Christian world is divided between the traditional and the experimental. It is divided between the past and the future.

Today Christians are faced with a choice between a past that will not die and a future that will not wait.

What are we talking about when we talk about a past that will not die? We are talking about a past that keeps sending out slogans such as, "Let's keep things like they've always been." A past that seems to infect policies and procedures with an idea of permanence. A past where a church stresses the familiar and comfortable. A past where the church seems to offer protection instead of exposure to the world. A past where the church seems to be stalling for time, trying to avoid controversy. A past where the church seems to have assumed the posture of people huddled in a shack out in the rain waiting for the storm to pass over—not realizing that entire civilizations have gone down the drain to ruin while the church postpones making certain decisions that could save it.

What kind of a future are we talking about when we talk about a future that won't wait? It is a future that is saying that the world

is on the move. Not only is the world on the move, but it is a
future that says that God is on the move. And, if God is on the
move, then Christians better be willing to move also.

Christians today must be willing to change their practices to
fit the changes of a new day.

Frankly, I have no desire to be a part of the past. Life is too
short and life means too much to me to be caught twiddling my
thumbs.

The question that I am concerned with as a minister of the gospel
is this: what kind of a Christian will it take to meet this future
that won't wait?

An International Christian

By international, I mean there must be no boundaries to the
extent to which we will go to bring people to Jesus. Pentecost was
an international revival—all nations were represented. All nations
had to be represented because that was the command of Jesus
Christ—to reach all nations. The Christian of tomorrow must be
an international Christian.

An Interracial Christian

Hopefully, we as Christians today, are becoming "color-blind"
in our efforts to reach people. The problem of race changes in
every part of the country. In the south, it happens to be a black
problem; in upper New York, it is a Puerto Rican problem; in
Oklahoma, it is a Mexican problem; in New Mexico, it is an Indian
problem; in Israel, it is an Arab problem. Wherever you find this
kind of problem, it is simply a refusal to accept the dominant
race at the doorstep in the name of Jesus Christ.

I have never been able to understand how we as Christians were
willing to send missionaries all over the world and yet remain so
blind with regard to people who needed Christ at our own doorstep.

There is no place in the world of tomorrow for a Christian who
shuts out one person regardless of his color. The Bible does not
say that God so loved the middle-class whites that he gave his
only Son. It is a hard fact that all across the world, men can love

everybody except their neighbor and that's the only thing God asks us to do.

An Interdenominational Christian

I do not mean by this that a Baptist church must give up it's heritage or a Methodist church must surrender it's doctrines. I simply mean that the Christian of tomorrow must put the saving message of Jesus Christ before his own church doctrine. Our job is not to get members of our own church; our job is to bring people to Jesus.

An Interpersonal Christian

By interpersonal, I mean that we, as Christians, must be willing to get personally involved in the needs of the people around us. We must be interested in not only saving souls, but also in saving lives. We must be willing to get our hands dirty with other people's problems. Many people are not so concerned about whether they're going to make it to heaven as they are whether they're going to make it to Friday.

The Christian of tomorrow must be willing to deal firsthand with people's problems.

I have a friend who was hunting one time in Colorado. In the distance, he heard someone calling for help. He began to move in the direction of the voice. As he got closer, the cry for help was louder. Finally, he reached the place where the sound was originating. He found that one of his hunting partners had killed a man.

When he had first heard the cry, my friend had been anxious to go and help. But, when he found that someone had been killed, suddenly the problem was greater than he wanted to handle.

This is the very predicament that Christians find themselves in today. We want to help, but we don't really want to help. We want to help, but we don't want to get our hands dirty. We want to help, but we don't want to kneel down beside blood and death.

What I am saying in this chapter is that we, as Christians, have to put aside our petty little programs and prejudices. We must be willing to think only of one thing—how we can bring people to Jesus.

Today, we Christians are standing in the arena like the Roman who had to choose between the lady or the tiger. Two doors were in front of him. The only difference is that he didn't know which was which. He didn't know which one concealed the lady and which one concealed the tiger. But today there is the door of the past and the door of the future. And we, as Christians, know which is which. We know which door faces the future and we know which door faces the past.

The door of the past is a door that, if a person opens it, he can remain the same. This door demands no sacrifices; demands no changes. Things can continue as they've always been.

But the door to the future demands a new kind of Christian.

And so we hear a voice today that is calling. It is the voice of the past. The voice of the past is saying calm down. It is saying hold on. It is saying go back. It is saying wait.

But there is another voice calling today. It is the voice that is calling for help. It is the voice that is saying hurry. It is the voice of the future. It is the voice of people who need Jesus Christ. It is a voice that will not wait.

11

The Tension of Evangelism

What I mean by the "tension of evangelism" can best be described by the words of Jesus when he said, "Be in the world, but don't be of the world."

After you become a Christian, you have three alternatives:

1. Isolation
2. Intermingle
3. Evangelism

King Solomon *intermingled*. He brought in foreign gods and corrupted the worship of the one true God. Later, during the time the book of Ruth was written, the Jews *isolated* themselves. They cut themselves off from the non-Jewish world.

Both Solomon, and later the Jewish people, lost their witness, but for opposite reasons. One by isolation; the other by intermingling.

Real evangelism takes place when a Christian can go out into the world and, instead of becoming like the world, can bring the world to Jesus.

The book of Ruth was written and put in the Bible to teach this very lesson regarding evangelism.

Naomi lived in Bethlehem. During a famine, she went with her husband to the land of Moab. Moab was a pagan nation. There they worshiped the god Chemosh, and offered human sacrifices.

While in Moab, one of Naomi's sons married a Moabite girl named Ruth. These two were married for ten years and then the husband died. Naomi's husband had also died.

The story tells how Naomi wanted to go home to Bethlehem. This is a beautiful picture of what happens in the life of a Christian who has been away from God. The real child of God *wants to go home.*

In the story of the prodigal son, he wanted to go home. He didn't want to stay in the pig pen.

Sons always want to go home; pigs never do. Pigs are already at home in the pig pen. But a son (of God) always wants to go home.

I know many Christians who are living in the pig pen. And I know some pigs who are trying to act like sons. In fact, I know many Christians who have one end of their rope in the Father's house and the other end in the pig pen. They go back and forth. But the real child of God will always want to go home.

Naomi had been in this heathen land for ten years. She had been up to her neck in *the world.* But the story points out that Naomi never became *of the world.* She never lost her testimony. And as a result, she was able to win her daughter-in-law, Ruth, and bring her back to Bethlehem.

In almost every marriage ceremony you can hear the minister quote words that Ruth spoke to Naomi when she said, "Entreat me not to leave thee, or to return from following after thee; for whither thou goest, I will go; and where thou lodgest, I will lodge: thy people shall be my people, and thy God, my God" (1: 16).

What you probably didn't realize was that this was actually Ruth's profession of faith.

Read that first chapter of Ruth carefully. When Naomi told Ruth she was going home to Bethlehem, Ruth said she wanted to go with her.

Naomi explained to her that it wouldn't work for several reasons. First, because Ruth would be a foreigner and wouldn't be accepted by the people. Second, Ruth would find a different religion from the one in Moab.

This was Ruth's reply (with my own editing).

"Look, Naomi, I know it will be difficult. But there is something I haven't told you. I have watched you for ten years. I have heard you pray to Jehovah God. I have seen you stay true to him. Something has happened to me. I have come to love your God by watching you.

"So maybe your people won't accept me, but they're going to become *my* people, because *your* God has become *my* God."

Ruth had been converted! This was her profession of faith. And Naomi brought Ruth home to Bethlehem; and she brought her home to God.

Later, Ruth met a man named Boaz and married him. They ultimately became the great-grand parents of King David. Think of it! Jesus Christ came from the family tree of David.

This means Jesus Christ was born because of a godly king named David. But David may never have been born if Ruth and Boaz had not married. And Ruth and Boaz would never have met if Ruth had not come to Bethlehem. And Ruth may never have been willing to go home with Naomi if she had not been able to accept Naomi's God. And she could never have known of Naomi's God unless Naomi had lived for God before her.

This is a fantastic chain of events! And they describe personally what it means to live under the tension of evangelism.

Let me put it this way; I know some Christians who are surrounded by people everyday who need Christ. But these Christians don't have anything to say because they have lost their testimony with the people around them.

They went *too far* into the world. They couldn't stand the tension of being in the world but not of the world.

I know some other Christians who have plenty to say. They have kept themselves isolated from temptation. They have walled themselves up like hermits and studied their Bibles and prayed. The only problem is that they do not have anyone to listen to them.

The Bible says of Jesus that "he came unto his own, and his own received him not." The Jews in the time of Christ missed him because they weren't looking for him. They weren't looking for anyone. They had isolated themselves from a world without God. They missed the greatest evangelist in history because they had refused to evangelize.

Now you can see why I will never give up my ministry on Bourbon Street. At any given minute that is as far into the world as a person can go.

I don't enjoy seeing people ruin their lives. I don't enjoy living among pimps and·homos and drunks and crooks.

I do enjoy spending time fellowshipping with Christian friends. If I had my way, I could do nothing else but feast on this type fellowship.

But I don't have my way. I am under orders to be in the world but not of the world. I am going to stay close to Jesus so that I can have something to say to those who need Christ. But I am also going to pitch my tent one step from hell so that when I speak for Jesus, there will be somebody listening.

This is the tension of evangelism. You can't bring them in unless you're out there among them.

12

Go After Them

The title of this book is *Bring Them In.* The thought occurred to me that there should be a chapter in this book entitled, "Go After Them." We certainly can't bring them until we find them. We can't find them unless we go after them.

I want you to look at the book of Acts. I hope that, before you finish this chapter, you will explore at least the early chapters of the book of Acts.

I love this book in the Bible because it is a book "On the Go." I am a preacher on the go. I have always been on the go. I believe that you can't witness unless you go.

The book of Acts shows that first young band of Christians as they began to move out to witness for Jesus Christ. This book has been called the Acts of the Apostles. I do not think that this is what the book is about. The apostles are listed in the front of the little book. After that, with the exception of three or four, the rest of them are never mentioned again.

Other people have referred to the book of Acts as being the biography of Simon Peter and the apostle Paul. I do not go along with this. We only have a little information about the lives of these men in this book.

The book is not simply a geographical description of how Christianity moved out. The book closes with Paul finally getting to

Rome but Christianity had already been in Rome for thirty years before Paul got there.

I like the book of Acts because, primarily it shows how these young Christians literally had to fight to get the gospel of Jesus out to other people. It describes how Christianity had to break through in order to get through Jerusalem—through Judea; through Samaria, not to them, but *through* them.

These first young Christian witnesses had to fight all kinds of problems in order to witness. We think sometimes that we have obstacles to sharing our faith. We don't have any of the obstacles that these guys had. They had to fight through all the narrow Jewish concepts. They had to fight the idea that religion was built by Hebrews for Hebrews.

Penetration

As I study these young Christian witnesses, I keep coming back to the word "penetration." What they did was more than evangelism. They had to penetrate some of the hard-core worlds that surrounded them. Today, when I think about going after people in the name of Christ, I know that I am talking about penetration. You see, there are all kinds of worlds around us. There is not simply one world; there are many worlds: the world of government, the world of entertainment, the world of athletics, the world of education, the world of young people, the world of business. All of these worlds are completely separate from each other in a sense. Each of these worlds has its own population.

The world of government is populated by politicians, lawyers, judges, elected officials, appointed officials. These people talk a language all their own. They have certain things that they share in common with each other. The world of government is a world all its own.

The world of athletics is a world all its own. It is populated with basketball players, football players, hockey players, sportswriters, newscasters, television commentators, and fans. This world operates all to itself. It is a very definite and specific world.

The world of business is a world all its own. It has signs and numbers and figures that have meaning for the people in this world. It is populated by stockbrokers, buyers, sellers, bankers, borrowers, loaners. This world has a language and a calendar and a season and a set of rules all its own.

The world of entertainment is a world all its own. It is populated by singers, actors, actresses, plays, movies. This is a world all to itself.

Now, Jesus told us to "Go unto all the world and preach the gospel." When I think about all the worlds mentioned above, I think we have to revise what Jesus said in this way, "Go unto all the *worlds* and preach the gospel."

How do you go about witnessing to these various worlds? You do it by the process of *penetration*. Let me explain what I mean. We have all heard that the recipe for tiger soup begins by catching a tiger. The way to witness to the world of government has to begin by getting inside this world. Now, if you are not already a member of this world, how can you ever witness to it? Very simple. I didn't say easy but I did say simple. You go and win a lawyer or a politician or a judge to Jesus Christ. Then you teach him how to witness to his own world. In other words, the only way to get inside one of these worlds for Jesus Christ is to win somebody to Christ who is already inside this world.

As a preacher, I don't really belong to any of these worlds. I am not a lawyer, or actor, or singer, or athlete, or businessman. I like to think sometimes that I am a little bit of all of these. But when I face the truth about myself, I don't really belong in any of these worlds.

And yet, Jesus Christ has commissioned me to witness to all of these worlds. I don't fret about the fact that I am not a card-carrying member in all of the various worlds that surround us. I'm just going to keep working at the job of trying to win a businessman to Christ and then help him witness to the world of business. Then I'm going to try to win another athlete to Christ and teach him how to witness to other athletes. Then I am going to try to win another entertainer to Christ and teach him how to win other entertainers.

Establishing a Beachhead

Another phrase that has become very meaningful to me with regard to the kind of witnessing we are discussing, is the phrase, "Establishing a beachhead." In a sense, that is what I'm talking about when I talk about penetrating the various worlds for Jesus Christ. Whenever you win somebody to Jesus Christ, you have not simply won that one person, you have also established a beachhead in his world. If you win a woman to Jesus Christ who spends all of her time with a garden club, you have not only won a woman, you have established a beachhead in the world of the garden clubs.

What I'm saying is, don't ever be satisfied with just winning a person to Jesus Christ! Realize that you have established a beachhead in some specific world. Help that person understand the world in which he or she lives. Then help teach that person to go into his own world and take the gospel of Jesus Christ. This kind of witnessing excites me like nothing else I can think of.

I am not going to sit around and fret about the fact that I'll never have an opportunity to be a famous lawyer. I'm just going to try to win another lawyer to Jesus Christ. Then I will know that my witness will be continuing in the world of law.

I'm not going to sit around and be sad about the fact that I'll never be a great professional athlete. I'm just going to win me another athlete to Jesus Christ and establish a beachhead in the world of athletics. Then I am going to teach him how to go and win other athletes to Jesus Christ.

This is what I mean by going after them. Maybe there will be times when the phrase "Bring Them In" won't work. If you win a person to Jesus Christ and he belongs to the world of business, you don't want to try to bring him out of that world. You want to help train him to witness to his own world for Jesus Christ.

I think sometimes this is where we throw cold water on a person when we bring him to church. That person lives out there in that world of his six days a week. We bring him down to the church on Sunday and try to make him enjoy a little unreal world of fellowship with a little group of Christians sitting around in a circle.

Down inside, that man is so uncomfortable he doesn't know what to do. He knows that when he leaves that church, he's going to have to go back out and face that world in which he lives.

What we ought to be doing when we bring him to church is training him to get ready to go back out in that world of his. We ought to let him know that we know how hard it is out there. We ought to help him anticipate the problems he's going to face. We ought to tell him to share what he finds in Jesus Christ with those people in his world.

So I want you to think with me as we continue to try to witness about the philosophy of witnessing by penetration. Let's go after them in the name of Jesus Christ. Let's go out there where people are who need Christ. Let's break through and establish a beachhead in their world. Let's win them to Jesus Christ. Then let's train them to help win those in their own world.

If you can understand what I am trying to say in this chapter, you can understand how I have witnessed on Bourbon Street. Many people have completely misunderstood how I go about witnessing for Jesus Christ on Bourbon Street. One person told me a little while back, "I think it would be the most depressing thing in all the world to spend all your time talking to drunkards and strippers and pimps and bums and all of the people that you think about when you think of Bourbon Street."

You would be surprised, for instance, how little time I have ever actually spent talking personally to strippers. Oh, I've done it about ten thousand times more than most preachers. But I haven't done as much of it as most people think I do. Here is what I do. I talk to one stripper and win her to Jesus Christ. Then I help teach her how to witness for Jesus Christ. After that, I just turn her loose to go witness to other strippers. I may not talk to another stripper about Jesus Christ for a month. But that one girl who found Christ is out there talking to strippers about Jesus Christ every single day. One of these days· there will be a knock on my door and there she stands with a couple of other girls that she's won to Jesus Christ.

When I win a bartender to Jesus Christ, I immediately teach

him how to talk to other people about Jesus Christ. I know that bartender isn't going to have to look for opportunities to witness for Jesus Christ. Opportunities are going to look for him. Opportunities are going to come and sit in those bar stools all up and down his bar. Opportunities are going to tell him their troubles. Opportunities are going to ask him his advice. I may not talk to that bartender again for two months. But I will know that during those two months, he's right there talking to others in the name of Jesus Christ.

Penetration! Establishing a beachhead! Going after them! This is what witnessing today is all about.

13

From Samaria to Gaza

The story of Philip in the book of Acts is one of the most exciting, enjoyable and beneficial stories about witnessing in all the Bible. It is the story of a man who had the opportunity on the one hand to preach to large crowds for Christ; but, on the other hand, he also accepted the challenge to go and become a personal soul-winner.

The story of Philip as a witness can be told with two words: Samaria and Gaza.

Samaria

So that you can get the feel for this story, let's look at what the Scripture has to say: "And Saul was consenting unto his death. And at that time there was a great persecution against the church which was at Jerusalem; and they were all scattered abroad throughout the regions of Judea and Samaria, except the apostles" (Acts 8:1).

"Therefore, they that were scattered abroad went every where preaching the word. Then Philip went down to the city of Samaria, and preached Christ unto them. And the people with one accord gave heed unto those things which Philip spake, hearing and seeing the miracles which he did. For unclean spirits, crying with loud voice, came out of many that were possessed with them: and many taken with palsies, and that were lame, were healed. And there was great joy in that city" (vv. 4-8).

First, let's refresh ourselves a little about Samaria. When you study the Old Testament, you recall the Hebrew people were taken into captivity by the Babylonians—by the Assyrians. They were taken to Babylon. Most of them were taken, but a few of them were left in the area of Jerusalem.

In order to populate the cities that had been left behind, the Assyrians sent some Assyrian people back into Israel to continue a community.

While the Hebrew people were in captivity, some of the Hebrews married Assyrians. Therefore, when the Hebrew people came back from captivity, they found three groups of people. They found a few Assyrians still there; they found some Hebrew people who had remained purebloods; but they also found this group of half-breeds. They began to call these half-breeds "Samaritans" because they had populated in the area just north of Jerusalem.

These Samaritan half-breeds became despised people by the Jews. The Jews would have nothing to do with them because they felt they had betrayed the cause by marrying Assyrians.

This breach between Jews and Samaritans was very strong during the time Jesus Christ was on the earth. For instance, whenever a Jew wanted to go from Jerusalem up to the northern part of the country around Galilee, he would always cross the Jordan River and go north and then cross it again after he got to Galilee. In other words, a Jew would do anything to keep from having to go straight through Samaria. They didn't want to get around these half-breeds. So the Samaritan people lived exclusively to themselves during the time of the New Testament. In the last chapter, we talked about penetration. But these people simply would not be penetrated.

Now, let's get down to what happened to Philip in regard to Samaria. You must keep in mind that during the New Testament times, the gospel of Christ didn't move about in a highly organized way. These young apostles and witnesses didn't meet together and say now here will be our plan for the next year. Instead, things were just exploding all around them.

For instance, after Pentecost, all kinds of trouble began to pop out. And the apostles of Jesus Christ were in trouble with the police every single day. However, the apostles had tremendous hold over the crowds of people around them and so the police couldn't get to them. The police were afraid to touch them. Instead, the police just began to put all kinds of pressure on the disciples. Therefore, in the middle of the night, some of the people had to literally scatter for their lives. They had to take the nearest road they could find and run up it. And that's what happened to Philip.

Philip was a young deacon. One of his responsibilities was to help feed the widows. Can you imagine what happened one morning? There was a knock on the door and there stood a couple of widows. They were griping and saying, "We don't have any food. There hasn't been anybody to our house to bring food."

Simon Peter would say, "Well, we don't bring food. That's what we have deacons for. Don't you know we had an election and said that we apostles weren't going to be carrying any more food to you folks?"

They said, "Yes, we understand that, but the deacons are gone. Everybody's gone."

Peter would probably ask, "Well, where have they gone?"

The widows would reply, "We don't know. Just the other day things got real hot and people began to close in on the deacons. They just had to strike out."

So this is what happened to Philip. In the middle of the night, the Jews were hot on his trail. He just had to jump up and strike out running. Now, he didn't have time to remember that he wasn't supposed to be going through Samaria. He was just taking the first road and that road happened to be the one that would take him directly north into Samaria.

I find this real amusing. I used to read in church history, when I was in the seminary, about how our missionaries spread the gospel of Jesus Christ across America. It always sounded so compassionate how our people were interested in taking the gospel of Jesus Christ into new places. One day I began to read some books that they didn't show me in the seminary and I found that part of the reason why Christian people left the territory where they were was because Indians were chasing them. And whenever they finally found a place where the Indians stopped chasing them, they would start a town and build a church. Thank God for the Indians! We might never have had the gospel of Christ down in the south.

This is exactly what was happening in Jerusalem. And this is what happened to Philip. Philip didn't exactly leave on a missionary impulse that night. He didn't say, "Well, I believe I'll go somewhere and testify." All of a sudden he was just grabbing his toothbrush and anything he could find and he was gone.

At any rate, the disciples couldn't find Philip anywhere. Anytime someone would come in from another village, Peter or John would ask, "Have any of you seen a man named Philip in your area?"

One day a fellow came through from Samaria. They asked him if he had seen a man up in his area by the name of Philip. He said, "The name doesn't sound too familiar to me but I'll tell you that things are really happening up there in Samaria."

The disciples questioned him as to what he meant. The man continued, "The whole town is down at the city auditorium. They are all down there. There is some guy preaching and everybody was listening. It's the most fascinating thing that's happened in a long time in that whole area." Peter finally asked the man if he remembered a name. The man said he couldn't. Then Peter asked what he looked like.

The man said, "Well, I couldn't even see him for people. People were all around him."

Peter continued to question him (as I see this in my mind while I read my Bible) "Could you hear him?"

The man replied, "I could hear him."

"Well, what was he preaching?" Peter asked.

The man said, "Well, the first night he was talking something about the prophet Joel. He was saying something about how some day the spirit was going to come and . . ."

Simon Peter broke in and said, "Why, that's old Philip! He's up there in Samaria preaching my sermons." Then Peter asked,

"What did he preach the second night?"

The man replied, "The second night, he had a sermon that was really a catchy one. He was saying something about tongues of fire."

Simon Peter stood up and said, "He's got my best sermon!" Then he asked, "What did he preach the next night?"

The man said, "Well, he preached the next night on how God uses us as a deacon."

Peter sat back down and said, "Well, Philip finally worked up a sermon of his own." Then he looked around at the other disciples and said, "Let's go up and see what Philip is doing."

So the Scripture tells us that Peter and John struck out for Samaria (Acts 8:14).

When they got there, they began to look around and they couldn't find anybody anywhere. They saw a little old man sitting down on the square and they asked him where everybody was. He said, "Well, the same place they've been every night. Down there at the city auditorium. They're all down there listening to this fellow preach."

So Peter and John go down there to the city auditorium and sure enough there was Philip right up there in the front. He had his Old Testament scroll, waving it in the air and he was yelling and pointing his finger and talking about Old Testament history and telling them about Jesus Christ.

Simon Peter stood there for a few minutes and finally said, "You know, he doesn't need any help preaching. Let's go around in back."

And so they circled around behind the auditorium. And, as people began to come forward wanting to know more about Christ, the eighth chapter of the book of Acts says that Peter and John began to do the follow-up work (vv. 15-17).

Now, don't you think this is exciting? Here is a man who was the preacher at the first great Christian revival in history—Simon Peter, the man who preached at Pentecost. And yet, here he is up in Samaria—the place he said he never would dare go—and here was one of his deacons preaching the first sermon he had ever preached in his life; and the whole city was responding to

Philip's preaching with great joy.

In other words, Philip, the deacon, was doing so well that Peter and John just went around and, as people came forward accepting Christ, these two apostles began to explain to them the deeper meaning of what it meant to be a Christian.

This is the first city-wide revival mentioned in the New Testament. Philip was the preacher.

Can you imagine how Peter and John began to tease Philip when the revival was over and they finally started back to Jerusalem? Can you imagine the ribbing they gave Philip? We know that they teased him because, until that time, he had been known as deacon Philip. But after the experience in Samaria, they began to call him Philip, the Evangelist. You can look in the twenty-first chapter of the book of Acts and it will say that one day they stopped at the house of Philip, but it does not add, "The deacon." The Bible says that they stopped at the house of "Philip the evangelist."

Gaza

Now, we are coming to the good part. Philip is now a popular city-wide evangelist. He gets almost as many invitations to preach as Simon Peter. He can go now to preach to any large group in the country because they all know he can handle the big crowds.

One morning Philip comes down to breakfast and just sits there with a frown on his face. One of the other disciples looks over at him and says, "What's the matter, Philip? Don't worry, you'll have another preaching opportunity. Everybody is crazy about you."

Philip sits there and says, "That's not my problem. I'll tell you what my problem is. All night long I kept waking up and I kept thinking about Gaza."

One of the disciples said, "Well, you better forget that. It would take you weeks to get down to Gaza."

Philip replied, "I know it, but I just kept thinking about the fact that I at least ought to get out on the road and go down toward Gaza."

One of the disciples again spoke, "Philip, there is not anything down there but a bunch of Philistines and there isn't anything between here and there but desert."

Philip said, "I know it. And I know that it sounds stupid. I don't know what's wrong. I just keep thinking about Gaza. So you fellows just take care of things for awhile because I'm going to start down the road toward Gaza."

Philip goes about five or six miles outside of Jerusalem down a barren road toward Gaza. There is nothing but desert on both sides of the road. There isn't a tree or a flower or a piece of grass.

But out there, in the middle of nowhere, there is an Ethiopian sitting in a chariot!

And when Philip sees this man, all of a sudden something in his heart tells him that's exactly why he's out there. So Philip runs toward the chariot.

When he gets to the chariot, this Ethiopian is simply sitting there with the Old Testament scroll in his lap and he's reading it.

And Philip runs up to him and says hello. In fact, he asks the man what he's reading. The man shows him and he's reading out of a book of Isaiah. Philip says to him, "Do you understand what you're reading?"

The man looks at him and says, "How can I understand unless somebody helps me?"

Philip climbs up in the chariot and sits down and looks at the book of Isaiah. The Scripture says that Philip "began at that same scripture and preached unto him about Jesus."

Boy, am I glad that was a deacon out there at that chariot instead of a preacher. If that had been a preacher, he would probably have begun talking to that Ethiopian about the historical background to the book of Isaiah. He would have begun to explain to him how the scroll was written in the first place. He would have explained to him that there are eight or nine critical problems in this part of the Old Testament. He would have told him that there was a possibility that there were two Isaiahs.

But you see, Philip didn't know anything about that. All he knew was that Jesus Christ had something for his life. If that Ethiopian had been reading out of the book of Leviticus, or the book of

Malachi, Philip would have done the same thing. He would have just gotten into that chariot and told the man what Jesus Christ did for him.

When Philip finished, the Ethiopian, who they say was a man of great authority, started his chariot moving back in the direction of Jerusalem. They went about two miles in silence and Philip didn't even know if he had gotten through or not. In a little while, they came to a well. In fact, today they still call it "Philip's well." The man pulled his chariot to a stop and said, "Can I be baptized?"

Philip looked at him and said, "Well, if you believe with all your heart, you can." The man looked at him and said, "I believe that Jesus Christ is the Son of God." And the two of them got out of the chariot and went down into the water and Philip—who had only preached his first sermon a few nights ago—baptized his first convert with his own hands. And the Scriptures tell us that Ethiopian got out of that water with great joy and climbed in his chariot and waved good-bye and turned that chariot in the opposite direction and disappeared down the desert road.

Isn't this a tremendous contrast we have in just one chapter from the book of Acts? On the one hand we have the record of one of the greatest city-wide revivals that occurred in Samaria—in fact, possibly in all of Christian history. I mean, in one night, Philip went in and won that city for Christ. Winning a group of Samaritans to Christ would be like going in and winning a group of Communists to Christ. That's the kind of thing that happened in Samaria as this one man came in and preached this great city-wide crusade.

That same man, the next week, was sent by God out into a lonely desert to find one man and help that one man to come to know Jesus Christ.

I think that through Philip, God was trying to teach those early Christians something. I think it was one of the most important lessons that they ever needed to learn. And today, frankly, I think it's one of the most important lessons we need to learn. He was trying to teach them that the two go together: the massive appeal and the personal touch. In fact, I believe with all of my heart that one cannot long be sustained without the other.

There are a lot of Christians who like to witness as long as there's a big group around and it's attractive and they are getting a lot of attention. But there aren't many Christians who are willing to go out to a desert place and talk to one person about Jesus Christ. But a real witness for Christ has to be willing to go to Gaza as well as Samaria.

I tell you, this story speaks to my heart. I spend almost every night of my life preaching to great crowds of people in my crusades. And I have to admit to you that I love it. Nothing thrills me like standing up and preaching to a large crowd of people and then watching them come to accept Jesus Christ.

But I also believe with all my heart that God wouldn't let Bob Harrington do that if Bob Harrington isn't willing to go to Gaza.

But that isn't a problem with me because I love to go to Gaza. I like to find people sitting in lonely places all by themselves who need to know Jesus Christ. I like to go up and sit in the chariot with them and tell them what Jesus has done for me. As long as the Lord keeps giving me strength, I'm going to keep going to Samaria and preaching to the large crowds for Christ. But I'm also going to keep going to Gaza.

God may let you go to Samaria. God may open the door for you to witness to large crowds for Jesus Christ. If he does, you go.

But God may not want you to go to Samaria. God may want you to go to Gaza. God may want you to spend your time finding one person who needs Jesus and tell him about Christ.

So, if God calls you to go to Samaria, you go. If God calls you to go to Gaza, you go.

14

The Chief of Sinners

To win certain people is to win an army. There are certain people, when they finally dedicate their energy and their heart and their talents to the Lord, who refuse to walk through the world incognito.

They change everything they touch. They cause everything where they go to come under the influence of the Lord Jesus Christ.

Now, when we talk about Paul, we are talking about the chief. We are literally talking about the chief in the realm of Christian history. He was the chief in the realm of *interpretation*.

Thirteen of our New Testament books were written at the hand of the apostle Paul.

Now, he didn't bring a new gospel, but he interpreted what Jesus Christ did while he was on the earth. We all understand the need for interpretation. We can see a football game on Saturday night. We think we know what happened, but we don't. We have to wait until we see the paper on Sunday morning and find out the first downs, and find out the penetrations, and find out who did what, before we actually know by close interpretation what happened.

This is what Paul did in our New Testament. Jesus Christ, while he was on the earth, walked the earth. He would say to people, "Come unto me, all ye that labor and are heavy laden and I will give you rest."

Paul said, "That is justification." So Paul was the chief in the realm of interpretation of the gospel of Christ. He was also chief in the realm of propagation.

Get out your map some time and look at Jerusalem and then look at Rome. Remember his three missionary journeys. Remember that what time he wasn't on a boat, he was walking by foot and realize the energy, not just the mind, but realize the energy over a period of years that this man expended with his hands and his feet. Few men have ever matched him in the physical stamina that he put forth propagating personally the message of Jesus Christ. He was the chief.

Paul was also the chief in preparation. After he became a Christian, the Scripture tells us that, from the time he gave his heart to Jesus Christ, until the time he began his first missionary journey was at least nine years and possibly eleven. He withdrew to the desert.

Now, immediately after we decide that we want to give ourselves to God, we want to see the results of our labor. We want to do something. We want to accomplish something. But Paul thought it was important to retire to a desert and spend a decade trying to *become* something! No wonder he knew what he believed when he finally came out preaching. No wonder he was sure of his convictions. But we want shortcuts. We want the whole thing in a bag if we are going to fool with it at all. We don't want to pay a price of preparation.

But Paul was chief. He has been chief all the way down through history.

We've only had about five major thrusts of Christianity in history; I mean where Christianity got a brand-new start. Paul led one of them when he swept Christianity across the Mediterranean in the first century. Then, 400 years later, a man named Augustine was sitting one day reading the book of Romans and he came across the passage that says, "Put on the Lord Jesus Christ and make no provisions for the lust of the flesh." That day he dedicated himself to Jesus Christ.

Eleven-hundred years later, Martin Luther, one day was lecturing on the book of Romans when, all of a sudden, that phrase jumped out at him, "The just shall live by faith."

Two hundred years later, John Wesley was listening as someone read the preface to Martin Luther's book on Romans. There, he found a new, spiritual dynamic.

So, when we talk about penetration, the conversion of this one man was without question the greatest victory that Christianity has ever won.

This man was one of the greatest intellects of his day. He had few peers in the realm of Greek culture, or Greek philosophy, or Roman philosophy or history, or Greek mythology, or the mystery religions. There was no stronger adherent to Judaism than Paul.

Here was one of the greatest foes that Christianity ever had. He was literally the persecutor. He was the protector of Judaism.

Here was a man, one of the highest ranking Jews of the first century, who had literally put scores of Christians to death. He set out for Damascus. He went with one purpose in mind and that was to see how many Christians he could persecute in Damascus. But, after meeting Jesus Christ on the road, he was led blind into the city and there he came to know Jesus Christ as his Savior. So thoroughly did he commit himself to Christ, that Paul himself became a marked man. The man who came to Damascus as a persecutor of Christians had to leave Damascus by being lowered over a wall in a basket because the Jews were going to kill him because of his identification with Jesus Christ and the Christians.

So the persecutor in a matter of days became the persecuted because of his identification with Jesus Christ and the Christians.

Now, I mentioned the fact that Paul could be called the chief in all of these areas. I use the word "chief" primarily because Paul referred to himself as chief. But he didn't refer to himself as chief of anything that I mentioned because it hadn't happened yet. But Paul referred to himself as the chief of sinners. He actually felt that he was the greatest sinner on the face of the earth; not because of negative sin that he had committed, but because he had actually given himself to the persecution of Christians and he had tried to stamp out Christianity. He did it in the name of religion.

We can look at Paul and realize how people can be religious and determined and be dead wrong. But here was a man whose logic was clear. Judaism was the religion. Jesus Christ was dead and it was sheer madness for anyone to believe that this crucified Nazarene could be the Messiah. Now, this little Christian group was threatening Judaism. Judaism had to be protected; therefore, the Christian group had to be stamped out. Nothing that anyone preached in a sermon could change him.

So, that day he set out for Damascus. He cleaned out Jerusalem except for a few of the apostles. Everybody had scattered from Jerusalem. So he started for Damascus. As he walked down that road, there are two basic things we should note about his conversion. One is that which is uniquely Paul. The other is that which is universal to all of us. The unique occurrence came as Paul was walking down the road. It was about noontime and an Assyrian sun is always hotter than hot.

But, all of a sudden a light shone from heaven that was brighter than any sun and it knocked everyone of them to the ground, but Paul didn't get up. In a moment, Paul heard a voice. Everyone else just heard thunder. Paul heard a voice. In that moment Paul looked up and asked a question, "Who are thou?" and he saw Jesus Christ. Now that is what changed him. It wasn't the light. It wasn't the thunder. But it was that Paul, on the road to Damascus, saw Jesus Christ. He literally saw him as he had been on the earth. Later when Paul lists the people to whom Christ appeared after his resurrection, he lists himself as one to whom Christ appeared. Paul saw Jesus Christ on the road.

Now, you say, "Isn't that a little special? I haven't seen him. I don't know of anybody else who has seen Jesus Christ. Do you mean he literally saw Him? Isn't that a little unique?"

Yes, it is. But that is just the way God does things. Because when God worked on Paul that day, he had a special thing in mind. I suppose you might call it election. That's what the Scripture calls it. God did a special thing for Paul that he didn't do for any of us. We just might as well realize that. Paul was a special case. But what God did was like a doctor who had discovered a cure for cancer and yet he knew he was going to die so he calls in a young doctor and he tells this young doctor the cure for cancer; not that the young doctor might keep it for himself, but that in turn the doctor might tell the world and save the world through it.

Well, you see Christianity had just begun and Christianity didn't merely need a lot of followers; Christianity needed a *champion!* It needed a pace setter! So God reached down and did a special thing to Paul.

But remember this. There is no one way that God works. God works in many ways with all of us. I imagine it would be interesting to discover how many different ways God has used to bring each of us to the road to Damascus.

For instance, I could name several different ways that God works and I am sure that all of us would not fall in the same category. For instance, if I were to ask you to describe your conversion experience, you might describe it in terms of an *unconscious experience.* You'd say, "I know I am a Christian. I know I love God. I know that the Lord is my Savior. I just can't remember ever having an experience. I grew up in a Christian home. It seems like I have always loved the Lord. I can't remember a time when I didn't love the Lord. I am not saying that I've always been perfect, I've made many mistakes. But it seems as though I have always loved the Lord."

You might feel as though yours would be an experience like this. However, you might say, "I believe God brought me to him through a *process of steps.* There were certain experiences that I had."

Maybe a loved one became ill. Or maybe you went to the hospital yourself. Or maybe you were put out of school. Each time that one of these things happened, it made you think of God. It made you realize that you needed God. But you didn't come to him. You didn't trust him. But each one of them brought you closer until the day that finally you came. You may have had an experience like that.

Now there might be a chance you could say, "My experience has been sudden. I grew up apart from religious training. I did not grow up in a Christian home. I did not spend much time in church. Then the day came when possibly through a revival or through a series of church services, I had a lot of preaching all at once. I had to consider this thing all at once. I realized that I needed God and I gave myself to him and it was a *dramatic experience.* I can remember the day and I can remember the hour." There will always be some persons who had an experience like that.

Then there would be others who would say, "Well, I can remember when I wasn't a Christian all right. In fact, I can remember a good long time when I wasn't a Christian. It has not been too many great dramatic experiences that have occurred. There haven't been any deaths. I haven't been in the hospital. I didn't have an accident. I just think that through the years as I heard preaching, and heard the Bible message, more and more I came to realize my need of God. More and more I came to desire it until gradually I came to a place where I committed myself to God." So, yours would be a *gradual experience* we'd call it.

I suppose many would fall into this category. Then there may be a possibility you have had an experience, and I know this isn't Baptistic but allow me to use the phrase, yours would almost be the experience of having had a *conversion* and then a *reconversion.* I shouldn't use those terms. Here is what I mean. You came forward and made a profession of faith to Christ early in life. Maybe when you were eight, nine, ten years of age you came and gave your heart to Jesus Christ. But as you grew, it didn't seem to make any difference in your life. You never seemed to be able to draw on its power. You just grew on up and life seemed to have the same old problems and you seemed to fall right in with the rest of the folks that didn't have the Lord anyway and you never were able to lean on that experience. But then later in life, maybe in your teens, maybe after you were married, you came to a second experience. And that second experience changed your life. And the meaning of that second experience set your course and today you draw strength from it.

And yet, if I were to ask you when you were converted, you wouldn't mention that second experience. You would still contend that you were converted back when you were eight because you brought all the faith you had to the Lord at that time.

You may feel like your experience was sort of an *unconscious affair*. By that, you feel like you love God and you are a Christian and yet you can't recall ever a time and a place and a date or anything when you had an experience.

You may feel as though there were *two or three crises* in your life that made you consider God that later on they influenced your becoming a Christian.

You may come up void of religious training and not in a religious background and you were confronted with the message of God in a fairly brief period of time and you had what you'd consider a fairly *dramatic experience* and you can remember the time, place, date, and the experience itself.

You may feel as though yours was a *gradual affair*. You can remember when you were not a Christian. You can remember giving it much consideration, and you finally came to the point that you did give yourself to God.

You may have made a decision early in life and seemingly didn't draw too much strength from it and later came to a second experience.

What does this mean? It means that God works in many different ways. There is no one way. God used one way with Paul. He used one way with you, one way with me. God has all kinds of ways to get people out on the road to Damascus and to get them down on their face, blind, and needing help.

That's the unique thing about Paul. He happened to have seen Christ.

But the universal thing was that wasn't enough because he had to have Ananias.

He had to have human instrumentality. He asked the Lord, "Lord, what would you have me to do?" and the Lord didn't tell him. He just said, "You go on in to the city, and there will be a man who will come to you and he will tell you what you need to do." And so as Paul was taken into the city, then it was later that Ananias came and told him the things he must suffer.

Now, I don't know who your Ananias was, but did you know there is not a single person who is a Christian who didn't have help from somebody? Somebody helped you. Somebody found you blind on a road and they led you to the light. Or maybe several people. But you didn't see it written on the sky. You didn't have a vision. Somebody helped you. Everybody has got to have his Ananias.

I wonder how many people around you are blind, on their face, bitter toward life, empty, in need, crying for help, waiting for you to come.

I am quite convinced that there are a few of us who could never imitate Paul if we wanted to. But I believe that there are many of us who could follow Ananias and find those in our cities who are blind and lead them to light.

Paul's Witness

There is one key area where we can imitate Paul; namely, the *way* he witnessed.

I have said repeatedly that a witness is simply one who tells what has happened to him. Did you realize that we have in the epistles of Paul, his account of his conversion experience repeated *three times?*

Here was one of the greatest theologians God ever put on the earth who couldn't keep from telling everyone he was around what happened to him when he met Jesus.

I wish we could roll back the clock. We might be walking down a road and we would look over and see Paul lying in a ditch half dead. We would go over and shake him.

He would bounce out of the ditch and say, "Hello, there gentlemen; why, I've been so close to heaven the angels kissed me. They wanted to stone me back there for preaching Jesus. I would have been killed if some friends hadn't lowered me over a wall in a basket."

We would say, "Paul, you don't have to do things that way. Why don't you calm down and try to get along with the city fathers?"

He would look at us and say, "How can I calm down? Don't you know what happened to me?"

"Why, one day I was going down the road to Damascus, and a light shone down from heaven!

"And a voice cried out of eternity! It was Jesus, men, and my life has never been the same! Good-day, gentlemen, I must go tell others what happened to me."

A few months later, we might be down at the boatdocks and there would be Paul standing in line for a ticket. We would go up and say, "Where are you headed, Paul?"

He would reply, "I'm on my way to Macedonia."

We would put two and two together.

"Sure, Paul, Macedonia is a place of great wealth. You are going over there to explore some investments for the future."

He would look at us and say, "Do you really think I would go to Macedonia just for my own interests? Do you think I would go anywhere unless God sent me?

"Men, if you think that about me, then evidently I never told you about the day . . . the day when I was going down the road to Damascus. And this light shone down from heaven . . . and this voice cried out of eternity. It was Jesus! And I've never been the same. Good-day, men, I must be on my way."

Finally, one day we would see Paul for the last time. He would be in a prison in Rome, awaiting execution.

We would say, "What are you doing, Paul?"

He would reply, "Hello, gentlemen; I'm going to heaven in a few minutes."

Suddenly we would be gripped by the fact that this great man was about to give up his life!

Frantically, we would say, "Wait a minute, Paul; you don't have to die. You can live! All you have to do is just give up talking about Christ."

He would look at us and say, "Do you mean you are offering

me either life or Christ? Why, gentlemen, for me to *live is Christ!*
And to die is gain!

"Why, you act as though I never told you about the day when
I was going down the road to Damascus. And a light shone down
from heaven. And a voice cried out of eternity.

"No, men, there is no choice for me to make now. I made my
choice that day on the Damascus road. And I've never been sorry
for a moment."

He would begin walking toward the block where they would
cut off his head. He would pause and call back to us, "Don't ever
be ashamed of the gospel of Christ!

Fight a good fight! Finish the course! Keep the faith! There
will be a reward for you—a crown for you—from your Father in
heaven."

God forgive us if we fail to witness. If we fail to tell others
about *our* road, and *our* light, and *our* voice.

15

Life Beyond the Grave

The most predominant subject in the New Testament is the subject of life extending beyond the grave. It is the most talked about subject in the entire new testament. Not only that, but Jesus Christ himself spoke of the place in eternity provided for people who rejected God in this life. Jesus spoke of the destiny of those who rejected God more than any other subject on which he ever spoke, except the subject of stewardship.

Revelation 20:15 calls hell a lake of fire.

Psalms 18:5 calls hell a place of sorrows.

Revelation 16:11 calls hell a place of cursing.

Revelation 20:11 calls hell a place of filthiness.

Revelation 14:11 calls hell a place of unrest.

Isaiah 33 says of hell that one's breath is a living frame.

Thirteen different times in the New Testament Jesus spoke on the subject of hell.

In Matthew 5:29 Jesus said, "And if thy right eye offend thee, pluck it out, and cast it from thee: for it is profitable for thee that one of thy members perish, and not that thy whole body should be cast into hell."

In Matthew 7:13 Jesus said, "Enter ye in at the strait gate: for wide is the gate, and broad is the way, that leadeth to destruction."

In Matthew 8:12 Jesus said, "But the children of the kingdom shall be cast out into outer darkness: there shall be weeping and gnashing of teeth."

In Matthew 10:28 Jesus said, "Fear not them which kill the body, but are not able to kill the soul: but rather fear him which is able to destroy both soul and body in hell."

In Matthew 13:42 Jesus said, "And shall cast them into a furnace of fire: there shall be wailing and gnashing of teeth."

In Matthew 25:41 Jesus said, "Then shall he say also unto them on the left hand, Depart from me, ye cursed, into everlasting fire, prepared for the devil and his angels."

In Mark 9:43 Jesus said, "And if thy hand offend thee, cut it off: it is better for thee to enter into life maimed, than having two hands to go into hell, into the fire that shall never be quenched."

In Luke 16:23, Jesus said, "And in hell he lift up his eyes being in torments."

The Bible describes hell as a place of torment, agony, loneliness, and sorrow.

Every word that represents ugliness, godlessness, emptiness, can be a synonym for hell.

There is not a good word that can be said about hell. Every word from the Bible on hell is negative.

Now, I think that it is very important that we try to understand what the Bible says concerning eternity. I think it is important that from a standpoint of love and logic that we try to understand those things that God has prepared for those who love him. But I think it would not be fair if we failed to try to understand what God has prepared for those who have rejected him.

Now, both heaven and hell are not only biblical but are logical. Just as light means nothing without dark, night means nothing without day, up means nothing without down, life means nothing without death, right means nothing without wrong, heaven means nothing without its opposite. And so I am going to do my best to try to give you what I feel is a biblical concept of hell.

You have heard of a view called universalism. We hear men who say that some day regardless of what a person felt on this earth, regardless of what a person believed, regardless of one's attitude toward God, some day out there in eternity, though there may be a brief period for correction, though there may be a brief transitional period, some day, some how, some way, every person who is on this earth will end up in heaven.

Now, this cannot be. It just cannot be. For if this is true, this will mean that God will have violated the very precious gift that he gave to us on this earth. And that is the *freedom of our will.* On this earth, God does not force me to love him. He does not force me to have fellowship with him. He does not force me to love the things he loved and to do the things he wants me to do. Would it be fair for God, who did not force me to love him, and have fellowship with him, in this life to turn around and force that love, and force that fellowship upon me in eternity?

No, God protects the freedom of our role in this life, and God will protect the freedom of our will in the life to come.

What Jesus told us about hell, that we can count on. Whether or not you believe it is your business. But from the Bible, this is what Jesus Christ told us. He thought we needed to know about the place in eternity for those who reject God in this life. He told us three things basically.

He told us who was not going to be there. By that, he meant God was not going to be there. God was not going to be there in *loving* fellowship. God will be in hell. His presence will be there. Try to conceive of a place where God will not be. God is everywhere. God's presence sustains all things. But he will not be there in *fellowship.* He will be there *in the awareness that someone has lost him.*

As a man said, in the Scripture, when he asked for help and God said, "There's a gulf between us. You fixed the gulf. I didn't fix it. We cannot come to you. You cannot come to us." God will not be there.

You say, "Well, is it any different from what we have on this earth then?" Yes, it is different. Let me show you how it is different. Now, for instance, all of us have some things in common. For one thing, we are all God's creations; whether we love him or

Three days after his conversion, Bob won his first person to Jesus—his own mother, Mrs. Robert Harrington of Brent, Alabama.

Bob says: "Here on Bourbon Street in New Orleans when things are happening, move in on them in the name of the Lord, and help BRING THEM IN!"

This night club was turned into a chapel and the Holy Spirit honored the Word of God as Bob endeavored to BRING THEM IN!

Mayor Don Schaefer of Baltimore, Maryland, makes Bob feel at home—and invites him back every year for a prayer breakfast.

Brother Bob being interviewed after he has spoken on the stage of a night club

Bringing Them In creates a mass audience such as this crowd in Baltimore, Maryland.

Bob and his "girls" — (left to right) Rhonda, his wife Joyce, and Mitzi—get together on the Campus of Baylor University.

Brother Bob always has time for people as he autographs books and records and chats with those who attend his meetings.

Wearing a hard hat, *Bob the Soul-winner* meets workers at a shipyard.

Bob on the go, witnessing as he goes

Bob adjusts his tie as he prepares to adjust the spiritual thinking of a civic club in Ohio.

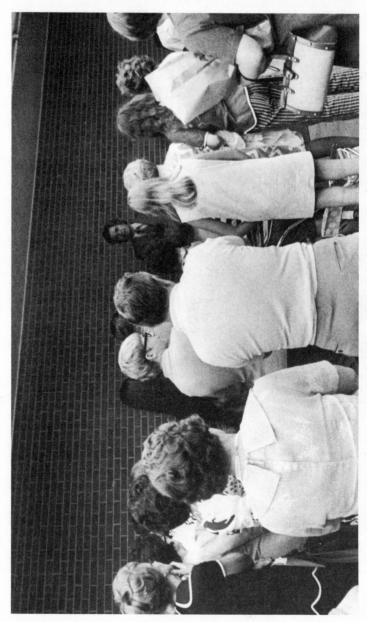

Bob Harrington, the *Bring Them In!* preacher, preaches in the parking lot of a shopping center.

whether we don't; whether we believe in him or whether we don't. We are all God's creations. God is behind all of our being here on earth.

Not only that, but we have something else in common. None of us has ever seen God. None of us has ever seen him in a vision. None of us has ever heard his voice, audibly. None of us has ever come that close to him. Our relationship to God has not been one of direct reality. But now there are some differences between us.

For instance, there are many of you who love God. This is what the Bible says. You love him but you have never seen him. You trust in him but you have never seen him. You pray prayers to him, but you have never seen him. You have lifted your voice to him, but he has never thrown his voice back to you. However, the Bible says that some day your relationship to God will be closer than it is today. Now, God will always be a mystery. Whether it is heaven or here. God will always be greater than we can understand him. We'll always pick our brains trying to figure out about God. God will always be beyond our concept. We will never be able to reach out and grasp him.

But the same God that brought heaven to earth in the form of Jesus Christ has promised that some day he is going to bring earth to heaven once again in the form of Jesus Christ and we will have a closer relationship with him.

But now what about people who do not love God? What about some of those of you who have never chosen to believe? You have never chosen to open your life to God. Well, even though you haven't, you are religious. You are religious whether you like it or not. Because you have religious friends, and you have religious loved ones, and you have available to you a religious book, and religious literature. You have become acquainted with religious songs. You have been in churches where religious things are talked about. You are a part of a society that draws many of its laws from a concept of the presence of God. Therefore, all of these things are around you and though you have never identified yourself with them completely, you draw comfort from them. You draw security from them. You say, "Well, I don't believe, but he does. I don't understand, but he does. I have never committed myself, but he has." And you draw comfort from the fact that, at any given moment, when you want it, God is at your disposal. God is within your reach. Therefore you put if off, knowing that it can be yours.

Well, the Bible says the day will come when at the same time in eternity that those who love God go into a fuller relationship with Him than they had upon this earth, that you will lose what counterfeit relationship you had with God: the friends, the loved ones, the religious environment, the comfort, the security, the identification. It will all be gone and you will be left without any identification of the loving fellowship of God.

Jesus told us who would not be in hell. God will not be there in a loving presence. *He told us who would be there.* In fact, he gave us a list, a very definite list of people. And after all, this is hell. This is eternity. You know the only important thing on this earth is people. Not buildings, or places, or temperature, or environment. But the most important thing on this earth is *people.*

Jesus Christ described a list in the book of Revelation. Let me just read the list. This list concludes by saying, "These are the ones who shall not be with God in eternity." He gives the list, and starts by saying the *fearful.* What the word means here is "people who are afraid"—not of life or things—but are afraid to talk about God. People who are afraid of the subject of religion. People who just don't want it to enter their minds. You have met a lot of them. I have people who will talk with me at any hour at any length at any place on any subject except religion. People who just don't want it to enter their minds. For some reason or another, they just don't want to give the subject a good solid battle through their own mental capabilities and their own emotions. They just don't want to discuss the subject. They just want to leave the subject completely alone. They are satisfied without it. Jesus said that those would be in eternity without God.

And then he says the *unbelieving.* Now, these are the ones who will talk about it, and they'll talk, and they'll talk. And they'll listen and they'll listen. And occasionally they will accept a part here and a part there. Like a woman walking in a supermarket will take *this* and put it back and then take *this* and keep it. They'll listen and they'll identify. But as far as ever committing themselves, as far as ever saying, "All right, it is mine and my life is on the line," they never do it. Unbelieving in the area of committal. Jesus said these people would be in eternity without God.

Then he says the *abominable.* The word "abominable" is a good word to describe as low as you can get. If you are ever trying to describe someone that seems to have so many bad characteristics that you can't think of anything good at all to say about them, just leave them in the category of the abominable. Jesus said that these would be in eternity without God.

Then he says the *murderers.* When Jesus referred to the murderers, he didn't just mean just anybody who had ever taken a life. This would include soldiers. This would include people who had killed accidentally. This would include people who had killed and were sorry for it later. This would include many exceptions. But what Jesus was referring to here was those people to whom life was cheap; to whom there was no reverence for human life; that even if he didn't actually kill, he *would* have killed if he had to, to get his way. Jesus said these people who never reverenced life at all would be in eternity without God.

Then it says the *whoremongers.* And once again, here Jesus is not referring to anyone who had ever committed an immoral act or had an immoral thought. But he was referring once again to that type person who never did care really at all what he did to someone's life; what he did to someone's home; what he did to someone's future. Throughout his life, the only thing that mattered was the gratification of his own appetites and his own lust and he did anything to anybody just to appease what he wanted for himself. Jesus said this type person would be in eternity without God.

Then the sorcerers he mentioned; the *cheaters.* Those people who go through life and never make an honest dollar, never say an honest word, never do an honest deed. Cut them open to the

core and there is a string of dishonesty about everything they have
ever done and said. Jesus said these would be in eternity without
God.

Then the *idolaters*—those that could only worship the things they
could see in this life. They had to touch it; they had to see it;
they had to feel it; they had to hear it; they had to know it in
some kind of definite, concrete way. But they could never hold
on to any idea that would go beyond this life. The idolater, the
worshippers of 'the things of this world, Jesus said would be in
eternity without God.

Finally, it summarizes by saying that all *liars* will be in eternity
without God. Once again, it doesn't mean just anybody who told
a fib. In the Greek language there are five different words for
lie. There's a word for a person who lies in business matters, one
who lies in family matters, one who lies in social matters, and
then one who lies in spiritual matters. This is the way it is used
in the second chapter of Revelation. The writer says, "And I know
that thou hast tested those who claim to be apostles and are not
and have found them to be liars." He was talking about those
people who had not only gotten inside a church, but had actually
worked themselves into places of leadership. To the outside world,
it looked as though these people were prime Christians, but in
their hearts, they were coated with hypocrisy and had never really
given themselves to God and their entire commitment was a lie.
So Jesus said that all liars would be there. None of these would
be in eternity without God because God put them away, but
because they had chosen a way of life and had never desired
anything else from God.

Now, you take that list and put it anywhere in your town and
then go out and move into a home and find out that you are
surrounded by that type person. You will move. You wouldn't
stay. And yet, this is going to be the make-up of eternity. This
is what the Bible says. I don't care where you put it. You can
put it on Miami Beach. You can coat it with all the luxury you
want. All the Bible is saying is that someday God is going to let
all of those people have what they want. In one place all of the

good people who rejected God are going to be at the same place together. All the horrible people who rejected God are going to be at the same place together and they are all going to wake up one day and realize that the thing they have in common is that all of them lived their life completely for selfishness. They never for one moment gave themselves to God. And they all are going to live there with the one realization: they had forgotten their souls completely and they are going to see in each other what they really have been in themselves and it is going to haunt them forever. For they will have been left to what they wanted.

Finally, God tells us how long hell will last. This is what the Bible says. Those people who spend their lives on this earth saying, "Leave me alone, God," God is someday going to leave them alone, to themselves forever! Jesus did make that perfectly clear. He made it clear that the way a person enters eternity is the way he would spend eternity. He made it clear that there would be no second chances beyond the grave. What good would it do? It wouldn't change your character. If you knew that you were going to have another chance beyond the grave, you would only put off what you are already putting off. It would only strengthen you in the procrastination and the way of life which is already yours. Once you finally got into eternity with a second chance you would only begin to think maybe you have a third chance or a fourth. It would be no good.

People say, "Well, that's not fair of God. We live on this earth such a brief time and we are here, we are gone. And then our destiny is settled. With him or without him, it just doesn't seem fair."

I would say that it wouldn't be fair of God if, when a little baby is born, real silently God would just drop a 1,200 question objective test into the cradle; not say a word, just drop it into the cradle. The understanding is that somewhere between now and the time that little baby dies; no extra merit for accident, disease, death, or sickness or anything. Sometime between now and death that little baby has to answer all those questions. They cover all the mysteries of life. They cover all the mysteries of God. They cover all the mysteries of the Bible. Very intricately, all of these questions have to be answered. Well, these little children grow up in their early years completely oblivious to the fact that there is even a test around that they're responsible for. They are seven- or eight-years old before they learn to read adequately. But still they don't have a way to know the seriousness involved in this test.

Finally, they come to their teens and they have been told about the test but they are so busy in other things and finally they get off to college and begin to realize the seriousness of this test. But already a third of their life is gone, if they had good health. So they get busy on the test and start into it. Before they get past three or four pages of answering simple little things about Sunday School and church and things they should have remembered but they didn't pay any attention to, all of a sudden they realize that at this rate they are going to have to live to be 150 to finish this test.

So they run down to the church and try to get help from their preacher and they beat on the door and he tells them to come in. They say, "Preacher help me. I'm on page 21 and I am stuck." He says, "Well, I am on page 64 and I am stuck. Get out of here. I am in a hurry."

Finally, the person goes and keeps trying to find the answers to the questions and little by little gray slips into his hair and he feels his health slipping away and he realizes that there are hundreds of questions still unanswered. He begins to cry, "Wait, God. Wait. You can't do it." Finally, an angel comes and tears the test out of your hand and the breath goes out of your body and you are doomed to eternity without God forever.

It would be unfair. It would be highly unfair. But you know and I know that is not what God has done. God has put us on this earth and he has given us every second of every minute of every hour of every day of every week of every month of every year. He has given us all of this time to answer one question. It is a question so simple that the youngest child could almost answer it today. Very simply, *"Will you love me and trust me?"*

Not, "Do you know all about me and can you explain me?" but *"Will you love me and will you trust me?"* And just in case we needed help on just that one simple question, very quietly God slipped a *Book* onto the earth and left it for us to ponder through all of its mysteries. There is a simple little message that God loves us very deeply.

Just in case we didn't understand the Book and the warmth wasn't transmitted, God made sure that there were some friends and loved ones around who would communicate this love so that we could feel it. Just in case we needed a little better direction, very quietly God allowed churches to open their doors and let you come in and feel for a few moments the impulse of God moving upon your heart. Just in case that wasn't satisfactory to you, God put down inside of you a conscience and a probing spirit to remind you that he was always near. Just in case this wasn't enough, one day like a mighty missile from out of nowhere God invaded this earth in the form of Jesus Christ. In the most dramatic example of innocence being snuffed out by wrong, God painted an amazing picture of his love that we should never forget.

So I say to you, it's fair. Because God is looking, listening, and watching, not for your treatise on theology. God is looking for a heart willing to open a tiny crack and just say, "Lord, help me. I believe. Help me where I don't believe. Lord, I will. Help me where I can't."

So the alternative has to be yours. I've got to be honest with you and tell you that is the reason why life is so exciting. Because you can say no. Whether you like it or not you have just a minute, only 60 seconds in it. It has been forced upon you, you can't refuse it, you didn't seek it, you didn't choose it, but it is up to you to use it. Just a tiny little minute. But your whole eternity with God is wrapped up in it.

No, my friend, you will have no excuse.

Every sermon you ever heard will be evidence against you.

Every prayer ever prayed for you will be evidence against you.

Every invitation you ever stood through will be evidence against you.

You will have no excuse for having said no to love, and life, and light—when God says:

"Go—where the worm dieth not and the fire is not quenched.

"Go—where the smoke ascends forever and ever.

"Go—where the ravens of despair sit on the hills of hell and croak out the doom in the pit of the damned."

And the only thing that can possibly put you there is your own willful, intelligent, deliberate, final choice to reject Jesus Christ in your life now—and forevermore.

16

Why We Must Keep on Witnessing

The following should be familiar to you: "When in the Course of human events it becomes necessary for one people to dissolve the political bands which have connected them with another, and to assume among the powers of the earth, the separate and equal station to which the Laws of Nature and of Nature's God entitle them, a decent respect to the opinions of mankind requires that they should declare the causes which impel them to the separation. We hold these truths to be self-evident, that all men are created equal, that they are endowed by their Creator with certain unalienable Rights, that among these are Life, Liberty and the pursuit of Happiness."

You recognize these words from our Declaration of Independence. There is a very close correlation between the words of the Declaration of Independence and the words in the book of Leviticus. When I hear these words, I turn in my Bible to the book of Leviticus 25:9-10 where it says, "And proclaim liberty throughout all the land."

This particular phrase, "Proclaim liberty throughout the land," was inscribed on the Liberty Bell, which, in 1776, rang in Philadelphia.

In 1835, the bell rang again. It was the funeral for Chief Justice John Marshall. And on that day, when the Liberty Bell was ringing, it cracked. As a result of that crack, it has been silent ever since. I think there is a symbol in the silence of the Liberty Bell. The symbol which I find in the silence also relates to the fact that I think that there is an untruth in the Declaration of Independence.

If it isn't untrue, it borders on being untrue. Let me put it this way; if it wasn't untrue in 1776, it at least isn't true for every generation. The untruth of which I speak, has nothing to do with the equality of men. The untruth of which I speak has to do with the phrase, "We hold these truths to be self-evident."

I contend that no truth is ever self-evident. The truths of the Declaration of Independence might have been self-evident to those men who were fighting for their own liberty and their own lives. I am sure that those truths in the Declaration of Independence were self-evident when Hancock, Adams, Sherman, Livingston, Franklin, and Jefferson penned their names to the document.

But if the spirit of 1776 were still just as self-evident today as it was then, we would not have all the problems of race and lack of patriotism that we have in the 1970's.

I, for one, think that today we need a renewal in our country of patriotism. Americans need to get such things as pride and loyalty and devotion out of the closet and dust them off and try them on one more time. It isn't that we, as Americans, ever gave these things up, but we simply assumed that everyone accepted them to be true. We assumed that the rights of human beings were evident. But we have had to learn as a nation, that even great truths are not self-evident. They have to be hammered out again and again in each generation. I think sometimes we have let this same thing happen to us in the Christian world. We have simply assumed that the truths are self-evident that all men are sinners and, therefore, all men need Jesus Christ. We have assumed that lost people understand there is a heaven and a hell and they must make a choice. We have assumed so much about the Christian life that we do not live out in our daily lives.

Most of us find ourselves in churches occasionally, singing the song, "Sweet Hour of Prayer." But how many of us spend an hour in prayer each day?

We sing, "Onward Christian soldiers, marching as to war with the Cross of Jesus going on before." But how many Christians today come around and volunteer for service. How many of you go to your minister and say, "Use me this next week. I want to do more for my Master."

We sing, "Oh, For a Thousand Tongues to Sing." Some of us don't even use the one tongue we have to tell other people about Jesus. I don't know what we would do with 999 more.

We sing, "There Shall Be Showers of Blessings." Most of us wouldn't even come to church if it was raining.

We sing, "Blest Be the Tie That Binds." And we let the smallest thing divide us.

We also sing, "I Love to Tell the Story of Jesus and His Love." But how many of you are telling the story?

I recall hearing a story one time of Christ returning to heaven after spending thirty-three years on the earth. The angels began to question him as to the plan that he left on the earth for seeing that his message reached other people. He told them that he had left a sufficient plan. Here was his plan: Christ said, "I left a few disciples; I told them my story; I lived my life; I died my death; I arose and left the truth with them; I left it burning in their hearts.

"They shall tell their friends. Their friends shall tell others and they shall not let it die. The angels began to question Christ and said, "But what if your disciples forget to tell? Or, what if they become too busy and do not have time to spread the message? What alternate plan do you have?"

And Christ admitted that he had no alternate plan—that one person would tell another person and that person would tell another.

This is why I think the phrase, "self-evident" is a dangerous phrase. None of us are Christians because the truth of God is self-evident. I am a Christian because other people told me the story of Jesus. They did not assume that I knew I was lost. They did not assume that I knew how to become a Christian.

Did you ever notice a phrase in the Old Testament that keeps cropping up again and again. At one point, the Bible will say, "A king arose that knew not Joseph." Another time it will say,

"A king arose that knew not Samson." What does this mean? It means that with every generation there is a sense in which the truths of that generation die with that generation. It means that, in the next generation, there must be others who are willing to tell the same story and tell it again and again and again.

I have in my files a sheet that lists the seven key rules to success in salesmanship. The last rule of the seven for being a successful salesman is this: "Tell your story again and again and again."

Television commercials are based upon one basic law: that a person will buy something after he has been exposed to that particular item at least nineteen times. In other words, the commercial world knows the value of repetition.

How then can we justify sitting around and refusing to tell the story of Jesus Christ? If I were convinced that the truths of God are self-evident, there would be no need for me to be a preacher. Every time the sun goes down, I am somewhere preaching because I know that people must hear the story of Jesus. They must hear it again and again and again, from you and from me.

17

Fishers of Men

I am going to confine this closing chapter to a more practical explanation about how to help bring other people to Christ. If you feel that you do not need any help in this area, then consider the book finished, and thanks for reading it.

However, if you think that it might help you to refresh yourself a little bit in terms of the doctrines, Scriptures, and methods of soul-winning, then this chapter should be helpful.

The Bible says that if we follow the Lord we will become fishers of men. In this chapter, I am going to talk with you about how I was saved and how I was called into the ministry; how I found the Great Commission to be palatable today and digestable today; what motivates me as a soul-winner; why I am a fisher of men; what it is like to be fishing for men. I remember when I got saved back in April 1958, in a little Baptist church in Sweet Water, Alabama. I never knew that day that I would become a fisher of men. This conversion experience leads to a lot of things down the road and we are not too sure what we will find.

Being a fisher of men, I never realized that the first soul I could ever win to the Lord would be my own mother, who gave me birth into this world. I was able to lead her into a new birth with the Lord. I heard my daddy introduce me not too long ago at the church where he is now pastor. I led my daddy to the Lord after I got saved and my daddy became a preacher even after I became a preacher. I have heard of son like father, but father like son is really quite an intriguing situation. So when you become a fisher of men, it is a wonderful compliment to be called a soul-winner. This is what I want to discuss in this chapter; not only about us being saved and others being saved, but how can we who are saved help lead other people to the Lord. Andrew, when he was converted, went to his brother Peter and led him to the Lord. This is how we share, by telling people what the Lord has done for us.

This thing about being saved, having a testimony, being born again is the most powerful weapon you can use as a fisher of men. Share with others the exact thing that happened to you. I don't have to argue about religion. I don't have to defend the Bible. I don't have to try to prove every verse to be inspired. I take it that way because I want to. I believe the Bible because I want to believe it. This is what happened to me on April 15, 1958.

I had spent my life in pre-med at the University of Alabama. I was a biology major with a chemistry and physics minor. I didn't know you could relate God to a person personally until that night I quit trying to figure him out and started faithing him out. If you can get a college professor of a skid-row bum to take the Lord by simple childlike faith, then you are going to have conversion. When you have conversion and follow the Lord, you will become fishers of men.

Being saved is one thing; then being called to serve the Lord is another. Somebody asked me when I was going into full-time Christian service. I told them that the night I got saved, I went into full-time Christian service. I don't believe there is any part time. I was licensed later to preach but until that time, I just boot-legged the gospel. I guess I was an illegal preacher, but I was preaching everywhere I could. I didn't know about all the licenses and ordinations.

Everybody's call is similar, but to everyone, their call is particularly peculiar. When I was called, I could not do anything except talk about the Lord. I was in the life insurance business. I couldn't talk about a ten-pay, a twenty-pay, or an endowment. I couldn't talk about any mortgage trust or anything like that. I would start writing an insurance policy on some guy and I would say, "Look, let me ask you if you are saved. Have you ever really been saved?" I even tried to get our insurance company to put two birthdays on the application. They asked me which one I was going to sell the premium on. They thought I was going to sell the premium on the new birth and that would be a cheaper premium. But my call was so clear. I wasn't on the road to Damascus, but I was in Sweet Water, Alabama. That call was so clear to me that I have never doubted in these many years that God not only saved me through Jesus Christ, but called me to serve the Lord in a full-time, twenty-four hour day capacity.

I got saved one day and three days later I was called. I hear some people talking about how they fought and fought and fought and finally surrendered. I don't know what it would have been like to fight a call. Man, when I got called, I was so tickled about being called and so thrilled to think that God called me that I didn't know you were supposed to fight that thing. I just surrendered. I went home and told my wife that I was going to preach. She said, "You're going to do what?" I told her again that I was going to preach. She asked me what I was going to preach. When I told her I was going to preach the gospel, she wanted to know what the gospel was. I said, "I don't know, but I am going to preach it." She said, "You're crazy." I said, "Well, pray for me that I'll get worse." I had a good, clear-cut calling and I told all my associates that I was going to preach. I stopped my real estate business. I stopped my insurance business and closed down everything that I had going. I went into full-time service for the Lord. I had no idea where groceries would come from, where clothes would come from, or shelter. But my wife, bless her heart, went back to teaching school during that first year of my conversion because somewhere some legal tender had to come in for food, clothing, and shelter. She went back to teaching school to help me fulfill the call of God because she found out that my salvation and my experience with the Lord was real. She wanted to move in like a good help mate and help make this thing more real. I thank God that I am not only saved, but I have also been called to serve the Lord.

The Gospel is the power of God unto salvation to all that believe and Jesus said, "Go into all the world and preach the Gospel to every creature."

In my conversion, there are three words that stand first, second, and third in my life. They are: Jesus, sin and go. Jesus took care of my sin and then He put me on the go. I have been going. I have a commission to go. God told me to go. Jesus told me to go. The Holy Spirit compels me to go. I don't believe you can grow unless you go. I believe you grow proportionately to the way you go for the Lord.

The reasons I have grown in the grace and knowledge in these few years is because I have been going. The Great Commission of the Lord says to go into all the world and preach the gospel to every creature. You can't spell God without go. You can't spell good without it, and you can't spell gospel without it. So I believe in that word "go" and I thank God that we can go. Everyone who is saved is supposed to go.

Jesus, even though he was God and man, was always on the go. He met Nicodemus in the night and Nicodemus was confronted with a direct witness for the Lord. But Jesus said, "You must be born again." Jesus was on the go when he met the woman at the well. He told her that she could drink the water he had and she would never thirst again. The early Christians were examples of people on the go. Everywhere they went, they went for the Lord. They went door to door, one by one and two by two. They went everywhere preaching the Gospel of the Lord Jesus Christ. We don't need any new methods today in witnessing. We just need to bring things up to date. We may use new written words, new ideas, and different thoughts, but the commission is still there. The "want to" should still be there. When we follow him, we realize that men are lost, men are condemned, and men are dying without

Jesus Christ. That is why, as Chaplain of Bourbon Street, I felt impressed of God and compelled of God to come down to the French Quarter of New Orleans and be a witness for the Lord Jesus Christ. My witness in New Orleans really does help my witness in the uttermost parts of the world when I go there because I try to practice what I preach at home and it works better when you are away from home.

Recently, in a night club in Dallas, Texas, the bouncer told me as I was coming in that was not the place for me. He said I should be in church. You know, that is an indictment on Christians, for the world to think that you are supposed to witness for Christ in a church. So now when you go out into the world, people think you are strange. I said, "Sir, you don't want me here, but God told me to come here and I have to listen to what the Lord says." A lot of people say they don't want to talk to their neighbor because they feel like they might be running them off. You're not going to run anybody off. Go witness to them. You may lead them in. This is the beauty part of the Great Commission. The Lord said to go and he would be with us, would never forsake us, never leave us, and he would bring everything to our remembrance. I think what keeps most people from going and growing in the Lord, is that they are afraid to. But something dawned on me one day when I was witnessing to this rough, tough man. I first told him that I was afraid to come see him and then he told me that he was afraid I was coming. Once I realized that he had a bigger fear of me than I had of him, I moved on in there.

As Chaplain of Bourbon Street, I would rather be alive and doing what I am doing today in this time that we are living in even though it is kind of sin sick, perilous, and corrupt. We have a bigger and greater opportunity to communicate the gospel than at any other time in the history of mankind. Just one day on television with Rex Humbard's Cathedral of Tomorrow reaches more people on Sunday morning than the disciples reached that first three years of their ministry. So it is a great time to be alive and to be a fisherman and a fisher of men. I thank God that I can appear to be what I ought to be for the glory of God; that

I can be armed with the tools that I need. I want to discuss right now how to approach people, how to witness to people.

You don't have to look like a hippie to witness to a hippie. You don't need to drink to witness to a drunk. You don't have to get hooked on dope to witness to a dope addict. You don't have to look dead to witness to dying people. When people are down, they want to look up. People who are wrong want to look right. People who are out want to look in. I don't think my doctor has to have cancer to tell me I have it. I don't believe I want to go to hell to let people know there is a hell. I don't think I have to live like the devil to let people know the devil will make you live wrong.

We need to communicate the gospel. We don't need to become relevant to the people we are dealing with. The gospel is relevant to the people we are dealing with. Down on Bourbon Street, I don't have to be a pimp to deal with those people. When I go to a city, I don't have to be a Hoosier to get their attention. All I have to do is lift up the Lord Jesus Christ. If I lift him up, not only in word and appearance, but also in deeds and makeup and know-how, and everything else, then God is going to bring people to the Father through the Holy Spirit.

I want to talk a little bit about the fisherman's equipment, the Bible. The Bible is a necessity to have in your witnessing. "Faith cometh by hearing and hearing by the Word of God." Even though we may memorize the Scripture, it is best to let the soul that you are witnessing to see the Bible, see it open and see the instrument in your hand. This is the reason the Bible is important.

The message today's fisherman has is the same message that the early fishermen had. It is what Paul told the jailor at Philippi. "Believe on the Lord Jesus Christ, and thou shalt be saved." Paul didn't talk about the doctrines of the church. He talked about the key to salvation. We don't have to major on the doctrines of the church or the deeper walk of the Christian life when we are dealing with a sinner who needs to be saved. Just tell them about the Lord, about salvation, and that salvation is simple faith in Jesus Christ. The Bible says, "For by grace are ye saved through faith;

and that not of yourselves: it is the gift of God: not of works, lest any man should boast." Thank God, salvation is a gift of God. So we need to tell them what Paul has told people all through the Bible, that salvation is to believe on the Lord Jesus Christ.

Closing the Witness

It's difficult for some to make the close—to lead a person to the Lord. They can talk about their testimony; but they have difficulty in closing out the prospect, to win him to the Lord. They have wooed him already, but they haven't won him. So, let's talk a little bit about that. Usually when I'm talking to someone, I say to them what the Bible has to say about all have sinned and come short of the glory of God and I point you, as the prospect, to the Bible. I let you look into the Bible. I turn with you and say to you, "Look at this verse right now." Then I'd ask you to read that verse aloud. "Would you say, please, sir, what is that right here?"

You: "For all have sinned and come short of the glory of God."

Me: Now that *all* includes you, doesn't it?

You: That includes everybody.

Me: All right, see now, here we are with the prospect. We've got you included in the fact that you are a sinner, but not just you, but I am too. We all are. Then I show you the wages of sin is death. Look at this verse right here, and read that for me (Rom. 6: 23).

You: "For the wages of sin is death, but the gift of God is eternal life through Jesus Christ, our Lord."

Me: Through whom?

You: "Jesus Christ, our Lord."

Me: You notice, it didn't say, through the church. It didn't say through the water; it didn't say through the sacraments. It said, "through Jesus Christ, our Lord." (I let them see that sin is a singular word. It doesn't have the plurality of sins.) All right now, the wages of sin is death. What is it?

Together: Death.

Me: "But the gift of God is eternal life." Now which one
            had you rather have? The wages of sin, or the gift of
            God?

You: Well, naturally, eternal life.

Me: Eternal life—all right now, how do you receive that?
            Over in Romans 10:19 it tells us how we go about
            receiving that. Now the next three verses, I want you
            to see and I've turned to the pages. It says, "That if
            thou shalt confess with thy mouth, the Lord Jesus, and
            shalt believe in thine heart that God hath raised him
            from the dead, thou shalt be saved." Thou shalt be,
            what?

You: Saved.

Me: All right now, the next verse says, "For with the heart
            man believeth unto righteousness." *(Usually about this
            point, you are saying, "Well, I have always believed in
            God; I've always believed in the Bible. I have always . . ."
            now that's the mouth believing, the mouth talking.)* The
            Bible says, "For the heart"—Say that word.

Together: Heart.

Me: "Man believeth unto righteousness and with the mouth,
            confession is made unto salvation." *(And all this time,
            the Holy Spirit is preparing the heart of that person and
            we've talked to them about our own testimony, about our
            own new life, and then comes the close-out verse, the most
            powerful of all if we had to name one that would be
            more powerful would be Romans 10: 13.)* "For whosoever
            shall call upon the name of the Lord shall be" . . .
            what?

Together: Saved.

Me: And that *whosoever*, that's you. Now let me ask you
            something. Do you believe this verse in the Bible that
            I am showing you right now?

You: Yes, I believe it.

Me: All right, read it out loud.

You: "For whosoever shall call upon the name of the Lord shall be saved."

Me: Are you a whosoever?

You: Yes.

Me: Do you want to be saved?

You: Yes.

Me: Would you trust the Lord as your Savior?

You: Yeah, I'll do it.

Me: Would you take him at his word?

Me: All right. Well, let me have your hand right now and I'm going to lead you in this sinner's prayer and I'm going to pray the prayer. You just ask the Lord what I'm asking him for you. You say this with me out loud when I lead you to that part in just a moment. Right now, I'll pray by myself. 'Lord, we thank you for the Holy Spirit that has worked on the heart of this friend. We thank you for Jesus who died for the salvation of all of us. We thank you for the Holy Spirit that's drawing this man to the Father right now, and Lord Jesus, come into his heart, forgive him of his sins, and save his soul. Help him when he opens his eyes and raises his head and he will know that he's saved because of his faith in the Lord and his belief in the word of God.' Say this prayer with me now.

Together: Lord Jesus (Lord Jesus) come into my heart (come into my heart) forgive me of my sins (forgive me of my sins) and save my soul (and save my soul). I believe in you, Lord (I believe in you, Lord) and I'm trusting you now (and I'm trusting you now) as my Lord (as my Lord), as my Savior (as my Savior). Thank you Jesus (Thank you Jesus) for dying for me (for dying for me) and help me, Lord (and help me, Lord) to live for you (to live for you). Thank you Jesus (Thank you Jesus) for saving my soul (for saving my soul) and help me Lord (and help me Lord) to live like I'm saved (to live like I'm saved) for Christ's sake (for Christ's sake). Amen (Amen).

Counseling at the Altar

I think one of the places that I have such a joy in being saved is just meeting somebody on the sidewalk or someone at the grocery store, or at the barber shop—and talking to them about the Lord. I've found the best way to talk to those people about the Lord is indirectly, which becomes directly. I talk about what's happened to me—how the Lord has changed my life; how important the church is; how important the Bible is. The first thing you know, you have "holy-whet" their appetite enough to want to relate and create a dialogue between the two.

When people come forward in my crusades, they're coming for one of two reasons—to be saved or to rededicate their life. I've always encouraged our counselors in crusades to meet them with this knowledge that they're coming to be saved or they're coming to rededicate their lives. And the Bible lets us know what to do with these two types of people.

I think at the altar, we don't have to repreach what the preacher has already preached. If a person's coming forward to be saved, we go ahead and open the Bible to Romans 10: 13, "For whosoever shall call upon the name of the Lord shall be saved," and if they are coming forward to rededicate their life, I John 1: 9 lets a person know that if we confess our sins to him, he is faithful and just to forgive us our sins. Thank God for this promise to us who are saved. A lot of times you get saved, then get bogged down in sin and difficulty, you just muddy your theological waters and your spiritual life is not up to date. Your prayer is not in tune. The Bible is cloggy to you—not clear. But he says, "If we confess our sins to him, He's faithful and just to cleanse us from all unrighteousness." That little word "all" is a powerful word. It's just three letters, but it means the world to me.

Now, this is important to me, to know that he not only has forgiven Bob Harrington, but he has forgotten my sin. And if that person who has come forward could see this, believe this and take God at his word, that person could leave that crusade, or that church revival more like he ought to be for the Lord and less like he's been being for himself.

I don't think any argument should be taking place during a counseling session. Whether somebody believes you can get salvation and lose it or get it and keep it, don't argue. If somebody believes in the gift of tongues, don't argue. If somebody believes in the baptism of the Holy Ghost differently from how you believe in the indwelling of the Holy Spirit, the altar is not the place to argue such things. The altar is the place for the Holy Spirit to disclose to a person's heart what he needs to do right then. I think the altar is more of a time to get close to the giver and not necessarily close to the gift. We need to recognize that when you are soul-winning at the altar, the main purpose is to win that lost soul to Christ, or to stir up the saved soul to live like he's saved for the glory of God.

Channeling the New Convert

As a full-time Southern Baptist evangelist, I travel around the country holding crusades across the nation, I'm always asked by people what about the follow-through. What about the follow-up. They ask about people, not only on Bourbon Street that we win to the Lord, but about the hundreds of people that come forward in my crusades throughout America. They ask, "What do you do? How do you channel the new converts?"

First of all, when they come forward at night, they are counseled by qualified, trained, prayerful counselors. Then we give them material and information. In exchange for that, we receive their name, their address, their church affiliation, their desires of future church involvement. From there, we hope to channel it into the churches, not necessarily of their choice. I can't make the general statement to a new convert to go to the church of his choice because a new babe doesn't know really where to go to get the food. I always like to recommend a Bible-believing, Bible-preaching church, one where the Lord is exalted, one where Jesus Christ is lifted up and the devil is rebuked; where believers feel the presence of the Holy Spirit; where they have a pastor who is a fisher of men. I believe we do an injustice to a person to get him saved and on fire for God and point him into a cold channel and expect to have him grow.

It is important from the start to teach him how to pray. I think it is difficult for a new babe in Christ to pray. I didn't know how to pray except "Now I lay me down to sleep," when I got saved. I had to kneel by the bedside with my wife and daughters. I'd hear my little daughters. They would pray for everything in the world; the bees; the dogs; and the cats. I heard little Mitzi one day thanking the Lord for the doorknobs on the house. I thought that was silly praying but then I got to thinking that that was real praying when you can talk to the Lord on a friendly basis like that. So I had to learn to pray.

I wrote earlier about a two-star general in Nashville, Tennessee, that I led to the Lord. Here he was, a man who had commanded hundreds and thousands of people. He was the Air National Guard Commander and he didn't know how to pray. I had to teach him how to pray.

I think in channeling these new converts, in addition to Bible study periods, you need to have a time to pray together. Let this person pray. If his prayer sounds amateurish, those are sometimes the most powerful prayers in the world—the prayer of a new convert.

I think you should take them witnessing with you. I think the reason most people don't enjoy growing in the grace and knowledge of the Lord is that they hit a bump and they get hung up. Or, they hit a place where they are afraid and they never break that fear barrier.

I think another thing we should warn the new converts is not to let little people bug them. Don't be annoyed by people that bug you. Don't put your faith in people. As a new convert I thought that everyone was supposed to be holy and everybody in the church was supposed to love the Lord. I had a rude awakening when I met some of the characters around the church. But hang in there with the Lord. Keep your faith in him. Encourage people and if you get hung up on a situation, back up and go around it. Don't let little things keep you from being the big thing that you ought to be for the Lord. Get involved immediately in your church, with your Bible, with your attendance, and with your giving. Become a tither immediately. Give of your time, your talents, and your money to the Lord and I guarantee that you will grow and go in the knowledge of our Lord and Savior Jesus Christ.

Conclusion

Many years before I was saved and called to preach the gospel, I had a negative attitude toward the church and God. I thought that when you came to the Lord, you had to cut out all these bad habits. I didn't know that when you come to the Lord, he would cut them out for you. I used to think you had to quit this, stop this, don't this. I didn't know about the start this, do this, go there. I didn't know the go things were there.

If people say, "Well, I'll get right with the Lord one day, but now I want to sow wild oats," I let them talk about those wild oats. Let them talk it. Let them talk about what they call good times and they will soon run out on the end of the limb. Then let us come back in with our good times. Ours are the only good times that are eternally based. It gets better instead of worse. They are the kind you want to rerun; the kind you want to keep on doing.

So I thank God that when I fell in love with the Lord, I found out that salvation is workable. It is palatable and it is "holy" digestable. The Lord is not going to hold you back; he is going to turn you loose. He is not going to make you endure your trip to heaven. You can enjoy it. There may be people reading this right now like that fellow listening to me. He said, "Bob, I was like you. I was playing church and I was a hypocrite and counterfeit." It is kind of bad to see yourself as you really are. When you talk to people about the Lord, they always say they are as good as so-and-so because they know which so-and-so to pick out. They pick out some dude that will elevate their ego and make them look a little better. But you know, the Holy Spirit puts you where you are. He lets you see yourself like you are and see yourself in your true condition.

Then I realized that I was a sinner. A lot of people who read this book know that they are sinners and they need to let the

Lord come into their heart, forgive them of their sin, and save their soul. I found out that the greatest call to Christ is a happy Christian, one who is a satisfied customer. A lot of people have heard me preach and said, "Bob, I want this Lord that you preach about." Even Paul was told by one of the leaders, "Almost thou persuadest me to become a Christian." If I have said something in this book that will cause you to want to let Christ come into your heart, forgive you of your sins, and save your soul, I hope and pray that you will do that right now. I am more than willing to ask you right now to pray and ask the Lord to come into your heart. Ask the Lord to come into your heart, forgive you of your sins and save your soul. Just bow your head and pray this prayer: Lord, forgive me of my sins, cleanse my heart, help me to love you, Lord, and to serve you better. Thank you, Lord Jesus, for dying for me. Help me Lord to live for you. Thank you, Lord, for saving my soul. Help me, Lord, to live like I'm saved. For Christ's sake, Amen.

I hope and pray that was your prayer today, that you asked the Lord to come into your heart just like I did on April 15, 1958.

Some popular, famous, wonderful words have been mentioned in this book. Words like Christ, Jesus, salvation and heaven. I think a powerful word is the word "go." That's a little word but it is powerful. So, by reading this book, if God uses it to help put more *go* in your gospel, it was more than worth it all. The Bible still talks about how a person can get saved. It says, "Believe on the Lord Jesus Christ and thou shalt be saved."

Thank God, I know that I am saved.

After leading his mother to the Lord, Brother Bob won his Dad, who is now pastor of a Methodist church in Alabama. Here Bob is with his brother Jerry and his Dad.

A scene from the set where national TV began for Brother Bob, "The Chaplain of Bourbon Street"